an
inspector
calls

a practical look at social care inspection

Graham Hopkins

illustrated by Stephen Hicks

Russell House Publishing

First published in 2000 by:
Russell House Publishing Ltd.
4 St. George's House
The Business Park
Uplyme Road
Lyme Regis
Dorset DT7 3LS

Tel: 01297 443948
Fax: 01297 442722
e-mail: help@russellhouse.co.uk

British Library cataloguing-in-publication data:
A catalogue record for this book is available from the British Library.

ISBN: 1-898924-57-0

Typeset by The Hallamshire Press Limited, Sheffield

Printed by Cromwell Press, Trowbridge

Russell House Publishing Limited

is a group of social work, probation, education and youth and community work practitioners and academics working in close collaboration with a professional publishing team. Our aim is to work closely with the field to produce innovative and valuable materials to help managers, trainers, practitioners and students. We are keen to receive feedback on publications and new ideas for future projects.

contents

dedication

for

Edward Kenny
who gave me the faith

and for

Kathryn Stone
who keeps it

acknowledgements

The hardest thing about writing this acknowledgement page is trying to figure how to weave in a seamless mention of Romford dog stadium (which is a bit of a motif for my books). So, having done that, I can get on.

Special thanks to Kathryn Stone, who inspects for England, for general all-round good egg support (even by an agent's standards) and for helping with the research and proof-reading, and commenting on the text. And to Sue Toole for ploughing through a draft and giving me more to think about (which I really needed with the book already some months late, thanks...)

Thanks also to the five case study units for agreeing to take part and for checking through drafts. Also, to those units that sent out questionnaires to inspectors and providers and, of course, all the people who filled them in.

Fourth and first-most thanks to the boy Hicks (Stephen by name, Stephen by nature) for illustrating once again how damn fine he is at all that drawing malarkey.

Thanks to Russell House (Mr and Mrs House's little boy) and his colleagues Geoffrey and Martin.

I would also like to thank wee Gordy for Moustapha Hadji, Youssef Chippo and Robbie Keane.

And can I just say 'hello' to anybody else who knows me.

Graham Hopkins

The author welcomes comments, rebuffs and questions on this book. He promises to try and respond personally to all letters. Please write to him c/o the publishers (address on page ii).

preface

The word *inspect* comes from the Latin *inspectus* meaning looking at, examination. If you look up the word in a dictionary you will be greeted with words like clarity, insight, perception, and observation. That should make inspectors feel good about themselves. However, look just a little harder and you'll see words like peering, prying, spying and surveillance. An all together more sinister gang of words that should make an inspector and provider shudder or, at least, feel somewhat uneasy. Inspection is a tricky word in a very tricky world.

Inspectors should see themselves as safeguarding, looking out for, watching over and taking care of people and things. And perhaps not as keeping tabs on or checking out. Inspectors have to gauge, judge, calculate, evaluate, assess, appraise, surmise, weigh up and ponder over, consider, reason and deduce. I have also had to do all those things while writing this book. I thought this would be easy. I was wrong.

It's my own fault for complicating things. Perhaps I should have just knocked out 30,000 words on the Graham Hopkins guide to inspecting. No, I decide to complicate things. First I consult with inspectors and providers. Thirty inspectors returned questionnaires, 12 heads of unit did likewise as did 118 providers (actually ten more arrived too late to be part of the statistical returns, but their comments have been used). Then I spend time with five inspection units as case studies, interviewing inspectors (23) and management (10). I spend time visiting homes, or rather my co-researcher did, inspected by the case study units to talk to residents (125), staff (27), managers (12) and owners who weren't managers (6). The picture I have is, in the great scheme of things, small. It would be foolish to claim the depth of this research to be definitive, but it is most certainly, I believe, indicative of what's going on out there. This book, in true inspection sense, is a snapshot of inspection.

As well as soap-boxing all my own ideas and thoughts on inspection gained from my seven years' experience at London Borough of Barking & Dagenham, I have also opened the pages of this book to the voices of inspectors and providers. So, hopefully it's not just about me giving it the big I-am and about how great Barking & Dagenham was (I got things wrong there, but I'm just not telling you about them), but a story of what it's like to inspect and be inspected, with ideas about how to improve things. And a story that is told – with a smile – in the hope of inspiring inspectors and providers alike. Back to the dictionary and you'll see that the word *inspection* sits in between *insouciant* (light-hearted) and *inspiration*. And that can't be far off being the best seat in the house.

face

As a lot of this book is based on my experience as inspector and head of unit (a sort of player-manager) at Barking & Dagenham, it might be helpful to explain a little about the set-up, which was, I believe, unique. Being a small borough (a population less than 150,000) the unit's remit was small. At the time I left the borough the unit had responsibility for 27 adult residential homes, two children's homes, one small home, about 40 home care services and the inspection only of children's day care.

Rather than employ full-time staff, we felt it would be preferable and manageable to contract out the inspection work. I was the only full-time employee of the unit and would do the registration and complaints work and manage any other add-ons (such as lay assessors). The use of contracted inspectors meant that not only could we bring in people with specialised knowledge and skills of the client group they were inspecting, but it also helped the unit to be seen by providers as independent.

From a management point of view this worked well. Every year targets were met. Inspectors only got paid if they worked and, strangely, I don't recall any sickness the whole time I was there. This also meant that I didn't have to pay things like on-costs, sickness, holidays and training. But on the other hand I paid well enough (inspectors would get about £1,000 per home), supported them well (I like to think) and got things done. I always came in on budget and the money saved would go on things like colour inspection reports, better publicity and so on.

Importantly, I was allowed (which I guess is the right word) to get on with things. The head of service with responsibility for the unit was inspirational and supportive, although for the last couple of years he was less around. The Social Services Committee trusted the unit and supported it (that is, didn't interfere). The unit worked and that was that. The leader of the council would whinge at times, the Chair of Social Services would label me a 'maverick' but the quality of the work was good, we were fair and that was that.

The unit's weakest link was with children's day care. The unit inspected services but the children's division had responsibility for registration and enforcement. It was a serious flaw. I thought it could work, but I was wrong. I believe that inspectors can be independent but all those involved in regulation need to be under the same management. To be not so is overly bureaucratic and a source of tension and conflict.

Nonetheless, the unit had a reputation for consultation and review, and an openness of approach and style that put people first, which two years on since leaving inspection, I am still proud of. As this book will testify.

post-face

how this book works

One of the things this book wants to achieve is help bring about improvements in the way people inspect. This means that scattered throughout the book will be boxes highlighting good practice. These have been chosen arbitrarily by me (hey, I'm out of inspection I can be subjective if I want): either because I think it's a good idea or because I have seen it work well for others. Sometimes it might be the idea that's good rather than any one unit's execution of it.

One of the curious things about inspection is that when you talk to inspectors about what they do, what is ground-breaking innovation for one is par for the course for another. Two examples illustrate the point. I was at a NAIRO conference in York one year when one of the delegates rose to say that after a long, hard consultation process, they are about to make inspection reports on nurseries open to the public. The NAIRO chair applauded this and said this was just what was needed, good innovative ideas like this. I had had nursery reports had been available to the public for three years.

Also, while visiting the inspection units as part of the case studies, I noticed that one unit used business cards. What a good idea, I thought. I hadn't ever thought of doing that. I'll plug that in the book, I thought. However, I discovered that all the units seem to have business cards, it was all a bit 'oh yeah, we've got them' run-of-the-mill stuff. So, I have looked to highlight the simplest things because while you might already being doing that, other units might not. There are also probably gangs of other ideas and innovations of which I know nothing and probably twice as many again that I have heard of but have forgotten. Apologies all round.

I have also listed things to think about to help with reviews of the inspection process. I hope you find them useful.

introduction

chapter 1 – introduction

I do feel inspection is a safeguard for residents and when I am old and have to choose a home, I hope it is inspected regularly!

manager of a private home

I personally feel that the inspection process is useful to residential work and should be something that is embraced – not feared.

owner/manager of a private home

More importance is given to records rather than residents in care.

manager of a voluntary home

Please *highlight quality of care and not solely hotel standards. We feel that our local inspection unit can no longer 'see the forest for the trees'. They are so bogged down in following set procedures and standards, and worry about 'dotted i's and crossed t's' in paperwork that they miss simply observing whether a home is a nice environment for care or not. We think they could simplify the inspection process down to simply speaking to staff, residents and family on a regular basis. After all, they are the ones that matter the most.*

owner/manager of a private home

Inspection is all about people. Or, at least, it should be. If there are no people to be residents, there would be no homes, no owners, no managers, no staff and, yikes, no inspectors. Astonishingly simple.

This book is about people. It's about what it's like being an inspector and what it's like being a provider. It is not, however, about what it's like being a resident. However, it is about how best to find out what it is like being a resident – whether you're an inspector or provider. I don't think any of us can *really* empathise with residents, but we can, at least, sympathise. It is hoped that if inspectors understand better the experiences and feelings of providers, and the other way around, inspection can be more positive, constructive, helpful and, in a word, effective.

My experience and research has shown that there is an expectation that inspectors instinctively know how to inspect. In the same way that inspectors (and everyone else in their everyday work come to that) are just expected to know how to write. But writing and inspecting are skills – and both can be practised and improved. And whatever the future of inspection, whatever tinkering takes place, whatever shape the promised Care Commission twist itself and regulation into, people will still have to inspect; people will still have to walk through doors. This book aims to explain and offer ideas about how to do that thing they call inspection.

I will bash my soapbox and stand on the table (I think) and show my colours from the off: I believe in inspection; I believe it is necessary and has great potential to be effective in not only making sure that people in homes at least feel safe and secure, but that it can help to improve the quality of life of people who live in homes. However, neither do I intend this book to be written on rose-tinted paper. There are undoubtedly good inspectors and bad inspectors. Just as there are good and bad providers. There are positive inspection processes and negative ones. It's the way the world turns. This book will try to highlight good practice as well as suggest ways to improve things. While not looking to criticise, it will look to be critical. And the critical voice will not just be my own, but also those of inspectors and providers.

One thing that never fails to amaze me is that despite working to the same laws, regulations and guidance, no two inspection units work the same way. Indeed, in some places, no two inspectors in the same unit work the same way. Some people (particularly, I would suggest, providers who have homes inspected by different inspection units) see this as a fault in the system and a bug to bear close to their chests; as proof of inconsistencies. I don't. Well, to be less clear: I do and I don't. Certainly some inconsistencies are baffling, but most are the product of local consultation, local needs and priorities, and are, in my view inevitable. We are talking about people, after all. And people don't simply fit into boxes marked 'A',

'B' or 'C'; nor do they sit comfortably on shelves. Pigeon holes are for pigeons not people.

A home may have 60 older people, but that doesn't mean that all those 60 think, feel or dream the same. Do older people dream? Have you ever thought about that? People are different: that's the thing about individuality – it makes people individuals. Being individuals gives people their beauty, but it also causes pain, anguish and suffering for those who like to label. The point is, I guess, that wherever people deal with people you are going to get those greatly feared 'inconsistencies'. Indeed, there would be something truly suspect (if not downright sinister) if every inspector worked in exactly the same way. A good reason, also, to be worried over the announced move of children's day care regulation to Ofsted.

No inspection unit would, I presume, claim to be perfect. Most, however, might point the first finger of blame not at themselves, but at their dire lack of resources (by which they usually mean money). Not their fault, you see, they'd love to be able to, but...you know how it is. No unit will claim to have enough time to do things the way they would really like. So, this means that the time spent inspecting has to be used as effectively as possible. This book aims to reflect and analyse how inspectors use their time, the tactics employed, and, wherever possible, to highlight good practice which other units or inspectors may either try as suggested; or try, adding a local twist (on the rocks, perhaps?).

Clearly as the author, I have my own views on inspection and down those roads I will drive this book. But being behind the wheel (which is worrying as I have no licence) doesn't mean that I will not listen to or try out a few alternative routes before arriving at the conclusion. This book is also about reflecting what actually happens at the moment – based on what inspectors and providers have said. There will be some things that if I was still head of an inspection unit I would not entertain, but clearly work well for others.

The style of the book, as you might judge from this introduction, is informal. Its aim is to be readable – certainly for all those who inspect and provide services (including lay people) and, maybe even for residents. It will be written in plain, everyday English – as you might expect from the man what brought you *Plain English for Social Services.* This doesn't mean (and it's sad that I even have to include this statement) that it takes the subject of inspection lightly. This is a serious book. But it tackles its seriousness in a very human way: even inspectors have been known to smile. Every provider and inspector seems to agree on one thing: you need a sense of humour to do the job. Well, I've certainly needed my sense of humour to write this book; so, it's only fair to expect you to use yours when you read it. Should you choose to dismiss this book because of its content, then fine: that's your right, you pays your money (thanks for that) you takes your choice. If, however, you dismiss it because of its style (not academic enough, not enough jargon, too patronising or too simplistic) then not only are we not singing from the same hymn sheet, we're not even in the same parish. And your hymn sheet is probably in Latin.

I don't know, some people...

being an inspector

chapter 2 – being an inspector

Warm, approachable, reasonable but also able to be firm, objective and decisive.

an inspector describing the ideal inspector

Someone who is approachable and talks to residents and staff and not at them. They should be seen as a welcome visit and not spread panic.

a manager of a voluntary home
describing the ideal inspector

My inspector is excellent ... I am very happy. My residents are not made to feel or even notice that an inspection is in progress. It is done in such a kind, friendly and interested manner.

owner/manager of a private home

---

at a glance

this section looks at:

the purpose of inspection

why people become inspectors

what it's like being an inspector

what providers think of inspectors

what qualities make for the ideal inspector

the most rewarding and frustrating things about being an inspector

introduction

Way back in 1991 when inspection units were set up, it's fair to say that they were partly staffed with people who did not choose to be there: those counting the days to their early retirements; those who were frankly so useless at their job(s) that even a social services department could not carry them any more (can't sack 'em? won't sack 'em! send 'em into inspection!); or, those who were working in sections that were subjected to a reorganisation, a restructure, a skill mix adjustment, or whichever weasel word their department had head-hunted from the macho-business-speak world of management consultancy to disguise the horrifyingly naked truth of a word like *cuts*. Hopefully, the passing years will have found out the motivation of these people and either they will have embraced the challenge or moved on elsewhere. Clearly inspection is a job but it isn't *just* a job. Is it? Not according to inspectors...

what is the purpose of inspection?

Inspectors were given five definitions of the purpose of inspection (see tables 1 and 2 below). Inspectors were asked to score each definition on a scale of 1–6, with 1 being very important and 6 being not at all important. The score for each definition was then added up and then divided by the number of people who answered, giving us an average score. Therefore the definition with the **lowest** score would be the **most important**. Here is how inspectors judge the purpose of inspection as *they actually carry it out at the moment*:

order	definition	score	average score
	inspectors grade in order of importance suggested definitions for the purpose of inspection		
1	ensuring that minimum legal requirements are met	50	1.67
2	protecting vulnerable people	67.5	2.25
3	improving the quality of people's lives	68	2.27
4	encouraging development of services	92	3.07
5	a job	124	4.13

Inspectors were also asked to score the definitions in the order of importance which, in their view, best defines the purpose of inspection as to **how it should be**. Interestingly, only four of the 30 inspectors graded each definition the same for how it was in their experience and how they believe it should be.

inspectors grade in order of importance suggested definitions for the purpose of inspection			
order	definition	score	average score
1	protecting vulnerable people	**43.5**	**1.42**
2	improving the quality of people's lives	59	1.97
3	ensuring that minimum legal requirements are met	59.5	1.98
4	encouraging development of services	74	2.47
5	a job	124	4.13

The purpose of inspection as being just a job is, as perhaps expected, was graded as least important to inspectors – not only as how it should be, but also how it actually is. Only one inspector thought inspection should be seen as a job and that that was how it was. That inspector said ' It's a demanding job and I feel it's important to remember that it is a job'.

It is also striking that inspection as a means of helping to improve the quality of people's lives was seen by inspectors as a very important part of what they actually do and of how it should be as well. One of the themes we will be exploring is the purpose of inspection: should it be a pure policing process, a developmental one or somewhere in between?

Overall, inspectors graded *the protection of vulnerable people* as the best definition of how inspection should be; and yet, felt that *ensuring that minimum legal requirements are met* was how their job was best described as it they carry it out at the moment.

why do people become inspectors?

Inspectors say why they became inspectors:

I liked the idea of being autonomous but part of a team.

The post of Principal Officer for the Elderly was phased out. As part of my work included registration and inspection, becoming an officer of the new inspection unit was the obvious course.

Enjoyed giving advice and guidance and felt well equipped to assess care practice.

Interest in quality of care and protection of vulnerable people.

I was asked to take the post by the Chief Nursing Officer.

Redeployment.

To pass on knowledge and experience to move residential care forward and to improve my knowledge of the workings of the Act and Regulations.

Concern regarding standards in residential care homes and a wish to be involved in improving same.

To improve practice in care homes.

To maintain standards, provide quality care and to protect vulnerable people.

The 30 inspectors who filled in questionnaires came mostly from management jobs within social and health care. Only two had held jobs previously that were not involved in direct care or social work. Their backgrounds were as follows.

the backgrounds of inspectors	
manager or deputy manager of a home	**15**
manager or principal officer in health or social services	**7**
social worker or care manager	**5**
personnel officer	**1**
training officer	**1**
independent nursing home consultant	**1**

When inspectors talk about why they became inspectors, their reasons could almost be filed away into three boxes marked 'to make a difference', 'to increase knowledge and take on a challenge', and 'redeployment or career change'. There was a sense that very few people judged inspection as a long-term career choice in itself; the impression being that inspection was a transitory, short-term profession: a sort of pit stop on the social and health care circuit. Indeed, one inspector gave the impression that inspection was something of a rest: 'Wanted to try something different still related to social work but not have the responsibility and stress of being a care manager/field worker.'

The feeling that inspection is a short-term career may be linked to the relative 'new-ness' of inspection and its need to prove itself as a profession with prospects. Or perhaps the strong focus given to personal development within local and health authorities instils into people the need to move and change in order to develop skills and knowledge. Or may be the uncertainty that has seemingly and endlessly hovered menacingly over inspection's head has not filled inspectors with enthusiasm over the chances of receiving the statutory Argos vouchers for thirty years' service to inspection. But it is an interesting comparison with providers (see Chapter 3: **being a provider**) who give the impression that, as long as it all works out all right, this is them for life.

To ensure standards were maintained or raised over a wider user group and to protect vulnerable service users.

To promote change and simultaneously attain new direction in career.

Desire to move away from operational practice.

An available job at part-time hours that matched my transferable skills.

To influence nursing and social care.

Hadn't worked for several years – used to inspect nursing homes, felt it was a good way of getting back into job market!

To share skills and experience, to be actively involved in promoting high standards in residential settings.

I hoped to improve the quality of life of people living in residential care and to ensure that homes adhere to the Registered Homes Act 1984.

I was looking for a change in job. The vacant post was advertised. I did not know very much about inspection then.

My job in personnel directly related to local authority residential care homes. I was asked to act up when the previous inspector left (before inspection units were formed).

Nonetheless, there are enough inspectors who remain upbeat, positive and still wanting to make a difference. One inspector said: 'I saw it as a job where I could have a direct and positive influence on the care of vulnerable people…' Another agreed: 'I thought it would be interesting and satisfying, a very direct way to influence care practice and protect vulnerable people.' One inspector interviewed said they became an inspector to 'Make a difference. Have an impact.' Not a bad advertising slogan, to boot.

Inspection units have also attracted people as a place to widen and improve knowledge, skills and experience. Perhaps with social and health care in perpetual flux and turmoil (who sound like solicitors), the feeling is that the generic will be more employable than the specialist. One inspector noted an 'interest in care of vulnerable people – keen to broaden my own experiences of the care sector and different client groups.' While another said: 'To enlarge my own experience. To move on from a comfortable environment. To (hopefully) affect the lives of a larger number of people.' Another said 'I wanted to have an active role in developing and promoting best practice standards. I also wanted to develop my own skills and knowledge-base and thought inspection would help me to do this.' This was the motivation for yet another inspector, who thought 'it would provide an interesting way of building on my experience whilst giving me the challenge of a new role.'

I do enjoy the way that social and health care take words, wash them down, polish them up a bit and send them out into the world. Words like 'challenge'. If a job is 'challenging' it sends out a message that it takes a special person to make a success of it. When, in unwashed, unpolished reality what it means is that this is one highly unpaid, thankless, bastard of a job. Similarly a word such as 'inappropriate' lends a sheen, a gloss to something which is plain 'wrong'. Hey ho.

While some inspectors looked to further their experience through inspection, for others it was their experience of inspection, either on secondment or as a provider, that propelled them into the profession. One inspector, buzzing with the thrill of it all, said 'My first experience of being inspected was very bland: did little if anything for me. However, my last inspection was a really positive experience. Even though my home didn't meet all the standards. But I felt at last I was getting good advice and support. So good that I wanted to be an inspector.'

Secondments have proved a happy hunting ground for some. One inspector said; 'Following on from a six month secondment I was hooked…' Another said: 'I spent seven months' secondment as an inspector. Enjoyed the change and challenge the role brought. After 20 years in residential care as head of home, I was ready for a change.'

Redeployment continues to play its role in staffing inspection units which, although it can be beneficial, does make one wonder about the independence of units that have to accept staff in this way. Staff are also recruited from outside of those with paid direct care experience. And thankfully so, I say. Well, I would, wouldn't I, because if they didn't I would never have been involved in inspection. Nor perhaps would this person: 'I love being an inspector. When I came back from maternity leave I saw this job in the Registration and Inspection Unit and knew that's what I wanted to do.' And if their effectiveness is but one tenth of their enthusiasm, then what more could an inspection unit want?

I wanted to influence and develop quality services.

what qualities should inspectors have?

the new recruits

I was interested in what qualities inspection units looked for when recruiting inspectors. To help with this section, I checked out **Community Care** magazine and **The Guardian** for adverts for inspectors. Occasionally I would phone up for an application pack. I did intend to fill in packs in different personas to see the type of interest I would receive, but I think I'll save that for the Care Commission.

Nonetheless, I learnt a lot just by asking for application packs. All the authorities I dealt with sent out the local authority's set pack: not one unit had designed its own application form or pack. Also all enquiries were to personnel sections and not the unit. This immediately tarnished any thoughts or perceptions of independence. I realise that this isn't always a choice for units and it is one of the problems of being part of a large bureaucracy. However, I do wonder how many units have even talked to their personnel sections about the possibility of taking care of their own recruitment and selection (suitably monitored for equality, fairness and other legal obligations).

In Barking & Dagenham, the inspection unit designed, sent out and received back application packs. The last round of recruitment I took part in (for children's day care inspectors) the selection panel included a councillor (who was a member of the children's advisory group), an early years worker, an ex-inspector, a provider and me. The personnel section monitored the process to ensure fair play. The fact that all the appointed inspectors had the last name Hopkins was purely co-incidental. I looked upon the unit as a sort of wholly-owned subsidiary of the council.

I decided to pretend that I was asking for a pack on behalf of a friend whom I called Ellen Gwynne (yes, I am so sad I even have to invent my friends) – and with that preferred spelling. Only one personnel worker asked me for the spelling of the name and all of them (yes, even the one who asked the spelling) spelt the name wrong. These people should imagine what it's like for them if their name is spelt wrong on something: at best it's embarrassing, at worst it's infuriating. If they can't even spell my name right...

Those that decided our Ellen needed a title of some sort plumped confidently for *Ms.* Now you see our Ellen has a thing about titles. She wants to know why it's so important to differentiate between her being married (solid citizen, probably a mother) and not (can't get a man, desperate) and *Ms* the one that tells you nothing except confirms the gender (but, hey aren't we right on sister?). So that makes a difference, does it? I hate being called Mr Hopkins – especially as my name is Perkins. But I do dislike the title *Mr.* I think it makes me sound like a demented cardie-wearing college professor. Which, of course, I'm not. Except the cardie, obviously.

The wording of adverts always puzzles me. It's almost as if there is a job advertisement governing body (wording and dullness) out there keeping everyone in line. Where's the innovation, the thought: this dross smacks of being knocked out in a 'will this do?' fashion. The only ad that I thought had something positive in came from Bristol. Its wording is a bit same-y and pretentious, and it is one rather overlong sentence, but the sentiment in my view is almost spot on. The second paragraph read:

> *The focus of the work is to ensure quality provision (the standards of service achieved and the extent to which these meet the needs of service users), the quality of the process of service provision (the premises, the management, planning and communications of service providers), and the quality of people providing the service in terms of their qualifications, training, recruitment and supervision.*

This gave a real flavour of what the job was about and made you think that the most important people are the service users – not least because they put them first. It would have been better to put staffing ahead of the building, but, hey, one step at a time. The only other example I'll draw came from Greenwich who wanted 'an exceptional and committed individual to head up our Social Services registration and inspection function.' Function? I say, old chap, what function do you head up? This must be even more bizarre for one inspector who said that the word 'function' is for them forever related to 'bowel movement'.

Interestingly there is a strong National Association of Inspection and Registration Officers (NAIRO) link for the cheapest and glossiest application packs. NAIRO chair Alan Jefferson's Lancashire lads and lasses clearly have a no-expense considered approach, while very little is spared for NAIRO life president 'Dame' Heather Wing's slick Surrey outfit. A north-south divide, perhaps. However, what Lancashire might not have in gloss (their application pack seems to have been produced on an old Corona), they make up for in essential social services pomposity: no sad old *job description* in the red rose county, they have a *Role Definition Statement.* Even Surrey's *Job Profile* is second division to that.

However, Surrey bounce back impressively by blowing Lancashire's *Core Responsibilities* of the job out of the water with their *Core Accountabilities*, *Sub-Accountabilities* and *Dimensions*. Sheer class. Packaged together in a glossy folder with a glossy inspection unit profile, a glossy social services profile, and even a glossy *Documents included in this pack* profile, I was gloss finished within minutes. However, all the good work was undermined by two fundamental errors. First, they sent dear Ellen an application to become a personnel assistant (no apology when this was pointed out) and second, and perhaps most fatally, their profiles include photographs (thankfully in black and white at least) of the senior management team and 'Other key senior managers' in full, uncensored toothy grins. A monumental error.

Actually, I was a tad unfair about Lancashire as their application pack was outdone for minimalism by the Metropolitan Borough of Wirral. A third of their nine sides of information concentrated on their smoking at work policy. Two sides detailed the policy and a third side was headed *Interpretation of Smoking Policy*. And when you've got policy sections headed *Original Base Framework for Agreement*, you'll see why the interpretation has been added.

The final word is, however, reserved for London Borough of Harrow. Ellen, bless her, phoned for an application pack on the Wednesday before the closing date (a bit last knockings, I know, but like anybody sticks to closing dates anyway). Eight days later, on the following Thursday a huge, bigger than A3 size envelope landed on the mat. Inside this Boeing 747 of envelopes was a compliment slip with a hand written statement telling the hapless Helen Quinn (whoever she was) that her request had been received after the closing date. I guess a moral here is, if you have an admin worker who is actually any good, love them, cherish them, bathe them in warm asses' milk, have their babies and pander to their every whim. It'll be worth it.

qualities asked of inspectors in recruitment

Inspectors were asked to score on a scale of 1–6 (with 1 being very important and 6 being not at all important) the qualities best needed to be an inspector. This meant that the smaller the score, the more important the quality. Inspectors scored the following qualities as follows.

what are the most important qualities needed by inspectors?			
position	quality	score	average
1	communication skills	43	1.48
2	inter-personal skills	48	1.65
=3	analytical skills	74	2.55
=3	knowledge	74	2.55
5	experience of managing services that are inspected	85	2.93
6	qualifications	90	3.10
7	experience of working in services that are inspected	93	3.20
8	experience of inspecting	116	4.00
9	experience of owning services that are inspected	160	5.51

Inspectors also suggested the following additional qualities: ability to work as a member of a team; the ability to self-manage (workload); a strong commitment to the values of care; an appreciation that inspection is/can affect people's business – i.e. commercial/business awareness; and objectivity to some extent.

It is very notable that the top two requirements are both linked, essentially, to the personality of an inspector, and the top four are all skills that can be acquired outside of working in social or health care. Qualifications and experience of inspecting score relatively lowly with inspectors. Owning a home, according to inspectors (and providers themselves – see below) could hardly be less important for being an inspector. Interestingly, working in a home is not considered as important or as desirable as managing a home. And yet, in my time, I've met more carers than managers who I thought might make good inspectors. Not managing a home shouldn't necessarily be a stumbling block, and inspectors seem to agree as it is only thought to be the fifth most important quality for an inspector.

We asked providers the same question. Here's how they scored it.

what are the most important qualities needed by inspectors?			
position	quality	score	average
1	communication skills	187	1.59
2	inter-personal skills	207	1.76
3	experience of working in services that are inspected	228	1.94
4	knowledge	233	1.99
5	experience of managing services that are inspected	239	2.04
6	analytical skills	325	2.77
7	qualifications	339	2.89
8	experience of inspecting	381	3.25
9	experience of owning services that are inspected	464	3.96

Other qualities suggested by providers were: capable of caring; conversant with staffing problems; understanding of practical constraints within specific client group; knowledge of client group; understanding of needs of people; fairness; sense of humour; objective/understanding; non-divisive inspection style; common sense; pragmatic/problem solving; preferably worked in both private and public sector at managerial level; attitude; ability to work **with** home owners; and an experience in the benefit system.

Providers, like inspectors, have communication skills and inter-personal skills as the two most important qualities an inspector should have. This, again, gives a strong message of the importance attached to the manner, style and approach of the inspector: can the inspector get on with people, can they talk to people and can people talk to them?

The third most important quality for an inspector, according to providers, was only considered 7th most important for inspectors: working in a home. This was closely followed by knowledge and managing a home. There is keen belief from providers that inspectors have some idea of what it's like working in or running a home. One of the sentiments here, I suspect, is that inspectors wouldn't come out with (what providers perceive as) petty comments, silly ideas or ridiculous demands if they knew what it was like to be on the receiving end of such things. It would root the perceptions of inspectors into the realities of running a home.

So, armed with all these qualities, what's it actually like being an inspector? In the next section inspectors tells us just that.

what's it like being an inspector?

Inspectors explain what it's like being an inspector:

There to support not nit-pick.

Got to be a people person but intuitive, vigilant and tenacious.

Interesting, stimulating, frustrating, tiring, exhausting.

Our joint working means that I can concentrate on the care of patients rather than environmental health.

Never dull – still learning after six years.

It's challenging, exciting and rewarding, but it can impose great personal stress.

It is never boring. Two days in a row are never the same. It can be challenging and stimulating and thought provoking. Above all it's enjoyable.

Pressurised – competing demands of caseload heighten danger of overlooking signs from any one source.

Although being an inspector (a good one, at least) is not easy, it is a much easier task to predict the type of words inspectors would use to describe it. Step forward: challenging, enjoyable, rewarding, exciting, frustrating, and stressful. Add that every day's different, the opportunities to influence and change, and the fun and games required in building, maintaining, improving or repairing relationships with providers and residents, and it's a fair bet that we've got all bases covered.

Indeed, this is pretty much the message from inspectors. There was plenty of positive thinking: 'I love seeing progress: home, managers and staff develop. I always look for good practice even in a home with the worse reputation.' Even the down sides help heighten the ups: 'Some days there's nothing good about this job. One phone call changes everything. You couldn't get bored with it. It's the only job that has held me in post this long [five years] without feeling the need to move on.' And there are those who, reassuringly for me at least, still feel a sense of privilege about what they do: 'I enjoy the job. I feel privileged,' said one; 'I enjoy doing it. I meet fascinating people. It's a privilege to walk into homes and spend time with them,' said another.

The continual sweet and sour emotions (the frustrations and the rewards) that baste inspection give it that special taste – and like all good specials, changes daily. As one inspector observed: 'Sometimes you feel that you are really working with a manager positively who wants to and are willing to improve the lives of their residents. Other times you wonder how a manager got their job as they are not able to understand or appreciate the impact residential care has on people and the loss of independence they face.' For another inspector it 'is sometimes worthwhile and heartening when practice is positively influenced by the inspection process. At other times it makes me angry when people's needs and requests are ignored. It is often scary.' Another said that they 'feel both a sense of fulfilment and frustration. When facilities work with inspection to move forward through negotiation and in partnership it is great. But the Act and Regulations can sometimes be difficult to implement.'

There was a very real sense of frustration over the ineffective and toothless (as some inspectors clearly saw it) 1984 Registered Homes Act. As one inspector said: 'Legislation is frustrating – open to

It is an interesting, stressful, challenging but satisfying occupation. No two days are the same...

Being an inspector is primarily a policing role...It means taking time to talk and listen, to show interest in that particular home, also respect all in it and act with integrity.

Very interesting – each home is different and it has been worthwhile to see the influence I have had...

Interesting, enjoyable, challenging, frustrating.

A position of authority, usually ensuring that one's opinion is heard and given due consideration. An excellent position from which to influence providers by working together.

Doing a job that most think is a good idea but rarely wants to be on the receiving end of. Generally a positive experience though.

I enjoy the opportunity to bring change but without the responsibility to be operationally involved in the change.

It is interesting and stretching – sometimes frustrating.

interpretation. We have a lack of clarity about how far you can push issues.' This was even more the case for those inspectors whose head of unit or whose authority were very unwilling to prosecute providers anyway. The effectiveness of units was felt to be diminished where those units relied on warnings alone. Warnings were ignored because no action followed. However, the experience of two of our case study units, Newcastle-upon-Tyne and, particularly, Suffolk are testament that if a unit takes legal action (which is fully supported by the local authority) then this has a resounding effect on how providers respond to requirements and recommendations made following inspections.

Enforcement work is the work of last resort. Threats of legal action should not be made unreasonably, but neither should they be empty gestures. Inspectors should be encouraged to work with providers who are failing to help improve services. Fair and reasonable timescales should be set, all reasonable effort made to work with someone on sorting out problems and concerns. However, this cannot be permitted to go on indefinitely. There has to be some positive moves made and action taken by the provider for this level of support to continue. If a provider rejects or ignores all support and guidance then reasonableness can be considered exhausted. The unit must then enforce and with the courage of its convictions. Although it is recognised that at times the politics of a local authority can prevent or frustrate this.

I don't intend to cover enforcement work in this book, but it is covered in the Department of Health's pack *The Briefcase.* However, suffice it to say that an inspection unit that wishes to be developmental also has to have the backbone to enforce as and when necessary. And to carry it through. The message will be heard loud and clear throughout your borough, city or county. As has been the Suffolk experience: 'Our approach has a different slant since the arrival of the senior – there is a point when you go into legal mode.' Another Suffolk inspector said the 'focus of my work has been on enforcement,' and that this had given them 'a sense of achievement' because they had become 'increasingly clear about my role'.

The feeling that inspectors could now carry out enforcement work (and mean it) and be supported throughout has helped not only confidence and clarity, but also increased job satisfaction. This is not because they have successfully prosecuted a bad provider (which is no mean thing in itself) but because the effect of this has boosted care standards elsewhere. Providers walking the tightrope of minimal standards have turned to the safety net of improving standards.

For many inspectors the key to success is the relationship with providers. In some cases this is more acute with 'private homes who are isolated – afraid of competition, they don't talk to one another.' Good relationships can help to avoid enforcement action as negotiation and support usually win the day. But inevitably this can never always be the case. And enforcement and confrontation are no

The job can be difficult, confrontational and frustrating. However, it is also interesting and rewarding as the inspector maybe the instigator of changes being made in promoting quality care.

At times very rewarding when you can see improvements resulting from inspection. At other times very frustrating when the opposite happens.

Mostly *it's a positive experience being able to work with and support homes in providing good quality care.* **Sometimes** *it's frustrating and painful, dealing with conflict and poor practice.*

Frustrating – at having to see how backward some people's approaches are towards their residents. Rewarding in seeing how small improvements lift the residents' quality of life.

An inspector is constantly challenging why things are done in a certain way.

The job is varied and interesting which helps to make it an enjoyable one. I have very good relations with most 'customers' and the mutual respect existing in most cases makes me feel both helpful and respected.

fun. As one inspector said: 'I don't like enforcement. It means that there has been a breakdown with relationship. Sometimes you feel like everyone is shooting the messenger.' Another said: 'I don't like confrontation: I handle it but I don't like it.' Also as inspectors' time is being crushed, then more time may be spent on higher risk places and less on others – affecting not only the relationships with those places but potentially stimulating (if that's the right word) cynicism in the inspector. As one inspector, who described the job as 'very stressful, sometimes satisfying', said: 'By the nature of the job more time is spent with people who are often running poor services and are antagonistic to inspection…potential to become cynical about carers.'

Nonetheless, confrontation and enforcement are the exceptions to the more positive norm. As one inspector said: 'So much depends on the relationship [with providers]. If you stick to pure inspection: you know, 'I'm the inspector and I'm here to tell you', you won't get very far… It has a lot to do with the right approach.' And 'the right approach' is the one this book is looking to define.

Inspectors who had previously been providers offered an interesting view of inspection from that side of the fence. And it's one, as can be expected, that has helped shape the way they carry out inspections. The most significant factor for them was that their inspectors were not approachable: the distant character, the aloofness, the lack of warmth. As one said: 'As a manager I felt threatened – didn't feel as if I could approach inspectors. Yes, you have a statutory role but staff should feel comfortable about contacting you.' Another agreed: 'As a manager experiencing inspection? I felt threatened at the beginning – nervous, anxious. Inspectors were 'professional' but a bit distant. I had no reassurance during inspection. The personalities and styles – the approach concerned me.' Similar concerns helped another provider-turned-inspector to at least know how not to inspect: 'I had to learn to cope with inspections. I was scared stiff of inspectors. I wouldn't do anything the way that I experienced inspection.' As did the approach of inspectors for this ex-provider: 'As I provider I worked in a hospital and had a varied experience of inspection: pop in for a cup of tea 'everything okay?' to full blown. The manner of nurses – it's that matron-y approach.' Another nurse inspector made a similar comment: 'Nurses are very tunnelled-visioned in looking at a care setting. They are oriented to hospitals and the medical model.'

The other experience invaluable for ex-providers is just knowing how demanding, worrying and draining an inspection can be. As one said: 'Inspection for me when I was a provider was an ordeal. I flapped around and prepared as best I could. Sleepless night the night before. You give a lot of yourself in the practice of care and so any criticism of your home you took personally. A good inspection and I feel as if they've approved my care.' Another said simply: 'Staff get spooked by inspection. We should remember that.' These experiences should help these inspectors carry out their jobs more effectively. Indeed, another positive aspect of being an ex-provider,

...it's very demanding, can involve confrontational situations and the discovery of distressing situations.

Very hard work using a wide variety of skills and operating in isolation.

is that providers respect the fact that they've done the job and know what it's all about. And this can be used to improve services, as one inspector said: 'It's nice for homes to speak to someone who's done the job. You can say things like: "It can be done because I've done it!"' However, experience isn't exclusive to working in homes, but also to using homes. As one inspector said: 'My mother was in a home for five years. That helped me to see a relative's perspective.'

While inspectors talked a lot about the variety and complexity of their role, there can be no denying that it can also be rather humdrum at times. As one inspector said: 'Sometimes satisfying, often frustrating but mainly predictable.' But perhaps the last word should go to the inspector who described being an inspector as 'my ideal job apart from being a cricket correspondent for *The Sunday Times* in the summer and rugby correspondent in the winter!' Any sport in a storm for some people.

R-E-S-P-E-C-T?
do inspectors feel respected?

We asked inspectors how they think they are generally viewed by various people. Inspectors replied as follows:

	well respected	mostly respected	partly respected	not respected
Users and relatives	7	21	1	0
Head of inspection unit	22	6	0	1*
Director of social services	7	13	3	1
Lay assessors	10	13	0	0
Private providers	2	19	9	0
Local authority providers	6	12	8	0
Not-for-profit providers	6	18	4	0
Elected members	4	10	4	1
Inspection advisory panel	9	15	3	0
General public	4	16	5	1

*The inspector qualified this answer by saying it was based on the previous head of inspection.

As with most questions that ask for general responses, the above was difficult for inspectors to answer. An inspector might well be very respected by two private providers, but despised by three: so, how to answer? However, despite this difficulty the overall picture is that inspectors feel, in very general terms, mostly respected for the work they do. Indeed, out of 300 possible answers only four found their way into the 'not respected' column. Inspectors also feel very supported by their heads of unit.

Some inspectors offered a few comments also. One inspector said that they were 'too well respected!' by the inspection advisory panel: obviously feeling that a more critical approach might be more beneficial to all. Another inspector highlighted what is surely a big concern for many inspection units – a lack of profile in the community: 'Public? Suspect many do not know of our existence.' And finally, one inspector ploughing their lonely furrows, getting on with the daily task of inspecting, remains the unknown inspector in the corridors of power: 'Director of Social Services? Probably doesn't know me! Elected Members and the Inspection Advisory Panel? They *don't* know me!'

the ideal inspector

OOKING FOR QUALITY? I can meet your standards. Woman inspector thirty something; qualified, skilled and experienced (in all areas) seeks care provider with GSOH and no previous requirements.

I suppose, strictly, if we did live in stalls at the ideal world exhibition, the ideal inspector would not exist. Everyone who provided care would do so with skill, love and enthusiasm. Vulnerability would be a word from a lost world. People would be trusted to care and repay that trust handsomely. All residents would have their place in the sun, living in clover on Easy Street where their days would be those of salad. They would be surrounded by bowls of cherries as they feast on milk and honey, travelling the fat of the land on the gravy train. They would sit comfortably all day in the lap of luxury and sleep well in beds of roses. And all would change their name to Riley. Now, that's a life. But not as we know it, Jim.

Sadly, in truth, we seek but to survive rather than live our lives. The sun is harmful, clover is fodder, Easy Street is now Skid Row, the salad's undressed, the cherries are unripe, the milk's gone off, honey became the title of a truly sickening song by Bobby Goldsboro, the land has become 95% fat free, the gravy train's hit the buffers, the luxury's all been lapped up, the roses have thorns, and Riley's life has died a death. Beam us up Scotty.

So inspectors are essential – or as a private owner/manager said 'a necessity to ensure "bad homes" are recognised and changed or closed if necessary'. But how do inspectors see the ideal inspector? Well they told us.

A competent person able to function alone, applying standards consistently.

I believe it is someone who is confident about their knowledge and commitments to the values and principles of care; who is interested and able to communicate with staff, owners, managers in a fair and objective manner.

Someone who is determined and tenacious, able to dig below the surface of what appears – but who can balance this by being polite, respectful and fair. A sense of objectivity and common sense are essential. Diplomacy in inter-personal skills and reporting also required.

A good negotiator with clear boundaries about what is acceptable and unacceptable practices.

Has a professional approach, good powers of persuasion backed by a good depth of knowledge. A good knowledge of the law, which can be flexibly applied in unique situations. Good at documentation and diplomacy.

A person who is clear thinking with good inter-personal skills who can assess situations and can establish a professional working relationship with a home. Someone who is prepared to challenge and take action as well as acknowledging what is positive and good.

*Objective, consistent, well informed, balanced in approach –
prepared to see both sides. Prepared to confront in non-
aggressive way. Quite courageous.*

*A person who likes people and has an understanding of the
stresses of caring… can maintain objectivity at all times,
communicates well and confronts issues in an assertive but
non-threatening way, can express themselves clearly in both
spoken and written word. Keeps up to date in own knowledge.*

*Qualities within an inspector: assertive, sense of humour,
approachable, inter-personal skills, negotiation skills.*

*Somebody who continues to try and improve standards while
working under difficult circumstances and who keeps focused
on quality of life issues rather than getting bogged down in
more technical issues.*

*The ideal inspector…has a good memory and doesn't make
mistakes.*

*An experienced social care practitioner who is fair, composed,
a good judge of situations and someone who is realistic about
'change'.*

*Someone who remains alert, vigilant, objective. Being able to
hold true to principles of good practice and the confidence to
confront any shortfalls observed.*

*A balanced, knowledgeable, professional with good verbal
and written communication skills who is unruffled in the face
of adversity.*

1. Is reasonable at all times and flexible, and not over zealous.
*2. Gets the annual inspection report and unannounced
    inspection report written up within 2-3 days!!!*
*3. Follows up requirements in annual inspection reports in
    accordance with agreed timescale.*
4. Works with home owners to improve standards.

*The ideal inspector is a skilful communicator – able to elicit
information with a professional friendliness from residents
and staff; to support and advise and not be confrontational at
all, in order to complete an inspection with the least
disruption. To be intuitive, thorough, persistent if required,
firm when necessary; knowledgeable re Act 84, constructive
with advice, approachable, sense of humour.*

*A person who can balance the inspection process in firstly
empowering residents but also working with the owners and
managers to achieve improvements over a period of time.*

PATIENCE and lots of it.

Need to be consistent and assertive in inspection and enforcing. Also recognise boundaries of own competence.

Someone who is honest, has a sound knowledge base, assertive, articulate and also enthusiastic.

The ideal inspector is a good listener with keen observation skills. He or she is honest and keeps up to date with, and has clarity about best practice. The ideal inspector is also a good negotiator.

the ideal inspector – providers have their say

I recall a scene in a television drama where an architect and builder disagreed about something. As the architect left the house being worked on he muttered 'bloody builders'; and the builder, left behind, muttered 'bloody architects'. I have in my mind this image of a similarly muttering inspector and provider: 'bloody inspector'; 'bloody provider'. I say this only because a strong purpose of this book is to encourage greater understanding between inspector and provider.

It should be very helpful for inspectors to see how providers think the ideal inspector should be (and in the next chapter, the other way around). To start with, we compiled a list of the words used by providers in describing the attributes of the ideal inspector. Here's what we found.

words used to describe ideal inspector	number of times word used
approachable, warm, friendly, pleasant, human, polite, good personality	43
understanding realities of a home, clients and their needs	24
experience	23
fair, reasonable	22
knowledgeable, informed	22
supportive, enabling, developing, encouraging, helpful,constructive, practical feedback	22
inter-personal skills, talks to clients, talks to staff	16

listener	**13**
open-minded	**13**
objective, non-judgmental	**11**
common sense, realistic, sensible, down-to-earth	**10**
respect, credible, offer and ask advice	**10**
communication skills	**8**
honest	**6**
assertive, firm	**5**
professional	**5**
sense of humour	**5**
compassionate, caring	**4**
flexible	**4**
recognise good work	**4**
sensitive, respectful	**4**
consistent	**3**
straightforward	**3**
thorough	**3**
calm	**2**
empathic	**2**
interested	**2**
knows the law	**2**
skilled	**2**
trusting	**2**
confident	**1**
don't take specifics out of context	**1**
dynamic	**1**
efficient	**1**
enthusiastic	**1**
gets to know home	**1**
good memory	**1**
good powers of observation	**1**
informative	**1**
intelligent	**1**
presentable	**1**
qualified	**1**

If this doesn't give inspectors a wake-up call, I'm not sure what will. By far and away the most important attribute for an inspector is their approachability (in all its guises). It scored nearly twice as many as the second most important attribute – understanding: another very human quality.

Although only mentioned by five providers above, a sense of humour figures prominently in many providers and inspectors' minds. Caring for people is a very serious business, but people are human, and we need to be able to smile and laugh with and for people. A good sense of humour (or gsoh as I'm told it's popularly known thanks to personal ads, which of course I wouldn't know about, oh no not me) is important to help you get through the stresses and demands of the day. But it is equally important as a means of communication. Making people smile and laugh, and laughing and smiling with them are great ice-breaking tactics. It also warms people to you, which means that they will be pleased to talk to you. Truly, in the caring trade, a sense of humour, in its place, is not be taken lightly.

Below we list what some providers had to say when asked to define the ideal inspector.

> *A good starting point is someone who accepts and understands that we can have a good day, a bad day and a bloody awful day – just like any family can have.*

> *Experienced in hands-on care, alongside administration. Willing to spend time to listen to the service users.*

> *Should have attractive personality as a cold, aloof, judgmental type sees only demerits. Growth only comes from the positive.*

> *Someone who is approachable and talks to residents and staff and not at them. They should be seen as a welcome visit and not spread panic.*

> *The ideal inspector appreciates the difficulties of running a home on a day-to-day basis. They would be approachable and a person you can ask for advice or help at any time. They should recognise areas where you work well above minimum standards.*

> *Someone working from the same benchmarks as their colleagues.*

> *Approachable person, who is willing to help providers identify any areas of weakness but highlight good areas of good practice.*

> *Someone who listens to both provider and user.*

Someone with common sense and an honest fair personality.

Ideal inspector should be approachable and congenial. They should be realistic in their expectations and fair in any criticism.

Thorough, interested, supportive.

Spends time talking to staff and residents

Fair, down-to-earth with a sense of humour and without an attitude problem.

Warm, friendly, quiet, respectful, helpful, informative, enthusiastic.

One who is able to ensure regulations and standards are being met, but is approachable and appreciates the realism of the job one is trying to do.

Somebody who is guided by the standards but is willing to look at what service the residents are actually getting.

One who knows what she/he is talking about.

A friendly person who gives feedback on relevant importances, not a person who only looks for faults.

Someone who smiles.

Fair, human, commonsense. Good inter-personal skills.

Now imagine that list on a person spec.

how do inspectors judge their success?

Inspectors, when asked how they judge their effectiveness, came up with five broad groupings. Their success is measured through:
- successful outcomes
- feedback from providers and residents
- management supervision
- managing their workload
- external audit

successful outcomes

Making improvements to services. Managing caseloads.

Improvement in the quality of services to clients.

Through what I manage to achieve in terms of better quality of care to residents/users of service.

Achieve change – improve quality of life for residents.

By the standards of the home, by helping homes develop.

On one level it's by gradually seeing and being part of improvements in care…

Effectiveness in influencing changes.

From our research, 'successful outcomes' was the most popular way of judging success, but is perhaps the most subjective and non-systematic way of doing so. Nonetheless, it is the one that undoubtedly gives inspectors the biggest thrill. For, make no mistake, having an impact that changes someone's life for the better is, indeed, a thrill. For both inspector and provider, it is what it is all about: it simply doesn't get better than that.

One inspector spoke for many when they said that they judge their effectiveness 'mostly from outcomes! Whether or not it has been possible to "make a difference" through the inspection process.' Two other inspectors reeled off similar sentiments: 'When over a period of time, I have convinced home owners and managers bring about improvements in their service'; and 'Whether I can work with home owners to improve the quality of life for residents.'

One inspector defined 'successful outcomes' as: 'Action specified is taken by proprietor. Enforcement action is successful. Enforcement action is avoided and practice is improved. On a personal level through supervision and appraisal.' Other inspectors linked in the importance of working with providers in order to have the influence to help change things for the better. As one inspector put it, a lot depends on 'whether providers perceive you as credible – do your observations lead to change.' Another inspector judged their success as follows:

1. *How much improvement or influence*
2. *How many requirements remain outstanding*
3. *How many operators use me as a sounding board*

Being used as a sounding board is clearly an indicator that the provider respects what you think and what you have to say. But surely for most, it is the inspector who believes that they are successful if 'as a result of my efforts, quality of life for residents improves' that speaks the warmest tones of job satisfaction. Throw another log on the fire.

feedback from providers and residents

The responses from managers who are providing a good service.

Many inspection units make use of quality monitoring forms to get feedback from homes on the performance of inspectors. This is an excellent method. However, some of these forms either just ask for general feedback or for more specific comment on a report. The more useful and instructive feedback is achieved if a specially designed form is used for commenting on how the inspector conducted themselves, with specific questions. For example, did the inspector turn up on time? Did they make clear the process that would happen during the day? Did they speak to you politely? How much time did the inspector spend with residents? Do you think that was long enough? And so on.

It would also help providers if they had standards against which to judge inspectors and the inspection process (see chapter 6 – **after an inspection**). However, this form of monitoring can be supplemented by verbal feedback gained at inspections. As one inspector said:

*My relationship with service users who actively seek me out
during inspections to talk to me. My relationship with
providers of care who feel comfortable asking for advice.
Feedback from proprietors in the form of quality monitoring
responses after inspections.*

However, one inspector rightly pours caution on relationships with
providers that become too cosy: 'You want to achieve a good
working relationship with home owners and managers etc, and work
alongside them, however, it is important that all parties remember
their role in this relationship and thus their responsibilities. Also, it is
important to develop rapport and good relationship with the wider
staff team and residents.' This cosiness usually sneaks up on
inspectors unnoticed – they think it's the fruit of many years work of
building up a relationship, but it can seem, no matter the innocence,
to be collusion. Counsel and Care in their report *Under Inspection*
refer to this as 'inspector capture'. It's a good phrase – I'll probably
claim it as my own one day.

Also there's a danger of inspectors being resistant to change.
They've got their workload: it's manageable, its sorted, it's safe.
They may be reluctant to give that up, fearing the unknown or
balking at the daunting prospect of basically starting all over again.
They may have spent some years building up a relationship only to
be told to walk away. That can be tough. But it is necessary. A
balance between good relationships and seemingly cosy ones has
to be struck.

Another inspector picked up on the importance of residents: 'If I
receive positive feedback where previously there was little, if any,
about changes in any aspect of the home, as experienced by
residents.' However, there seems to be little thought being given to
find out what residents think of inspection and inspectors, and how
they can effectively influence the process.

management supervision

Under 'management supervision' we can group target-setting and
achieving, feedback from colleagues, and supervision. Peer respect
is strong among inspectors: what fellow inspectors have to say
about each other is an important way of judging their success. As is
through supervision with management. For one inspector this was
exactly how they judge success: 'If I meet my goals as discussed in
supervision and with my colleagues.' Another inspector said for
them it was 'through consultation with line management
(appraisals).' Another said they judge success in two ways: 'By
charting progress in delivery of care to residents. By regular
supervision by manager of the Registration and Inspection Unit.'

To rely on supervision alone is perhaps missing out; unless, of
course, a supervisor has accompanied the inspector on inspections
or has collated monitoring feedback forms and is able to discuss the
way they work. Appraisals systems can also have an important role
to play. It must be beneficial for inspectors not only to have number

targets but also a means against which to evaluate their practice and their effectiveness – and appraisals offer that opportunity.

managing their workload

Feedback from owners and managers, and colleagues and line managers. Getting through the workload, delivering on deadlines without compromising too much on quality.

A more mundane, but important aspect of judging effectiveness is whether or not an inspector can manage their workload. It might not seem too tough a task to visit, say, 16 homes twice a year. But, as ever, bare statistics do not tell the whole story. Inspectors are also (mostly) required to register homes, investigate complaints (an increasingly bigger part of the job) and so on. If an inspector is involved in enforcement work this can take up all their time. Indeed, many inspection units fail to meet their target number of inspections which, as with anything, is understandable in some cases and not in others.

However, sheer numbers can tell a story if the number itself is especially high or low. No matter the difficulties an inspector can be expected to manage comfortably anything up to 15 homes. On the other end of the scale, once an inspector's workload passes the 40 mark, then there must be very real pressure on meeting targets. The bigger the workload the more likely that complaints and other investigations will also take their toll. The most obvious effect of a heavy caseload is the actual time spent in a home will be limited. Inspections suddenly have to fit in with schedules rather than schedules fitting in with inspections. Carrying out the required **number** of inspections may well be a performance indicator for a unit, but there should be a way of measuring the quality of an inspection as well as the quantity. Inspectors could spend 15 minutes in each home, meet the target and be praised by the Audit Commission and Social Services Inspectorate in a joint review as a well performing unit. Whereas, in reality, it is simply a dangerous one.

It's hard to quantify what should be a manageable workload. It's not just the number of homes but the size of homes that needs to be taken into account. But given that an inspector has a cross section of large and smaller homes to inspect, I would suggest (and that is all it can be) that 25 homes is a manageable workload. Beyond that difficulties and pressure will heighten, below that will allow more inspector time to support services effectively as well as regulating them. The national average is about 37 homes at the moment. That tells its own story, I think

external audit

One inspector spoke of external audit. They said they judged their success 'through our unit's accreditation to BSI [British Standards Institute 5750 – now replaced with the European standard ISO 9002]. This includes the inspectors being inspected and regular audits of practice by the unit manager and other team members.' It doesn't hurt to have such things, but I wouldn't rely on it alone. Of all the available awards, I think that the Citizen's Charter would be the most beneficial and relevant one for inspection units as the required standards are, at least, very public service oriented.

the most rewarding and the most frustrating things about being an inspector

the most rewarding

We asked inspectors to tell us what was most rewarding about being an inspector. And they did.

Knowing my experience can protect vulnerable people from abuse and poor treatment. Seeing homes and managers improve and develop.

Visiting a home which is operated and run well, where staff are confident, working as a team and where residents have a high quality of life.

The positive relations that I have with the vast majority of homeowners, managers, staff and residents – closely followed by the satisfaction of turning round or closing a bad home.

Help an establishment to move forward/change and improve standards.

The variety of residents and how small changes can raise their quality of life.

Feeling that you can 'make a difference'.

Seeing improvements.

Assisting facilities to improve and move on. Producing a good succinct report.

Promoting good social care practice and uncovering and exposing bad practice.

Seeing staff teams take ownership of changes that you have recommended.

Building a relationship with reluctant proprietor/manager, which enables change for the better.

When a previously ailing home moves forward in a positive way, no matter how much input that may involve the inspector initially.

...knowing that inspection, despite all its faults, does offer some protection to vulnerable people.

When the manager/staff suddenly understands what you're saying about improving the service they offer, and puts this into practice which results in improved care for residents.

...knowing we have contributed to many improvements in services. Having this acknowledged by managers.

Similarly we asked inspectors what is the most frustrating thing about being an inspector. Again they told us.

Lack of change in, for example, local authority services.

Dealing with mediocre services with managers who see no need to develop and improve those services.

The slowness of change and some establishments just meeting minimum standards and not particularly bothered about improving.

Difficulty in accessing user views. Limited contact with services.

The failure of the legal section to support proposed action.

When owners and managers do not understand the need to empower residents.

When home owners ignore (consistently) advice and hinder the progress of inspection.

The fact that reports do not reach a wider audience.

It is very frustrating when proprietors consistently disregard their statutory obligations and say they are 'too busy caring' to do it.

Writing endless reports.

Writing long boring reports.

Not having enough time to always complete development work.

Legislation focuses on inputs and not outcomes of care.

Bad practice, bad practice, bad practice and the inability of owners and managers to recognise it.

Workload, which impacts on the quality of the inspections. Could be more thorough.

When you have spent hours during an inspection in describing for people who should know the principles of good care practice and their importance – and you go back six months later and find yourself having to have the same conversation as though it had never happened.

The unreceptive home owner or manager who thinks they are the best.

Where establishments strive for the minimum, only just achieve this but perceive themselves as offering a very high quality of care.

When a home is in difficulties it's very frustrating to visit over and over again, all the time trying to encourage positive action and feeling that no improvements are being made. When inspecting you have contact with staff and residents, and the personal aspects are in your mind when enforcement action is being taken.

As with those of the providers in the next chapter, it is really worthwhile listening to what rewards and frustrates inspectors. It helps get into their minds and understand them better. I trust just letting inspectors have their say has gone some way to achieving that.

being a provider

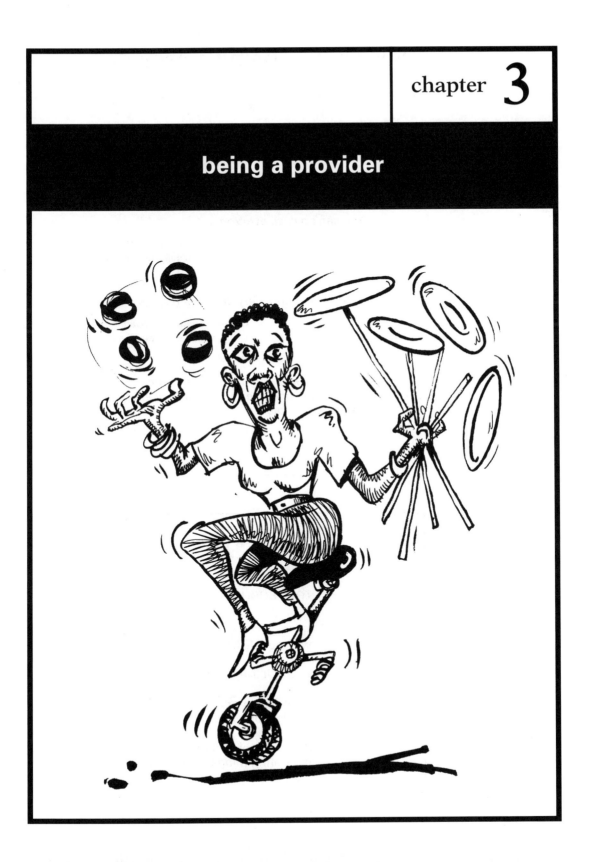

chapter 3 – being a provider

Under fire and under valued.

> owner/manager of private home on
> what it's like being a provider

You can't please everyone.

> owner/manager of private home on
> what it's like being a provider

Very demanding. Very stressful but rewarding.

> owner/manager of private home on
> what it's like being a provider

*One who has enough resources, time,
imagination and energy – but above all – treats
people as people.*

> a provider describing the ideal provider

---

at a glance

this section looks at:

why people become providers

what's it like being a provider?

what would make someone
an ideal provider?

the most rewarding and
frustrating things about being
a provider

why do people become providers?

Understandably, when asked why they became a provider, most people said that they wanted to care for, work with or provide a better quality of life for their particular client group. Many managers and owners said that they had experience in caring and had worked up through the ranks. For one it had become a family tradition: 'My wife is a nurse and my parents also had a home. It seemed natural to carry on caring.' Those last three words seem like a good title for something.

Other providers said they wanted to make a difference, wanted to be their own bosses, wanted to give something back to the community or were fed up with lousy standards and wanted to do better themselves. Not one provider said they were in it for the money. I raise this because I think it's important and helpfully controversial. There is for many people, inspectors included, a feeling of unease about making money out of caring for people. For some it's hard to swallow and always leave a nasty taste in the mouth. Because of this private providers may be viewed as the baddie riding desperately to the bank to deposit another bag chockfull of their ill-gotten gains.

I have to admit (many years ago) I used to have suspicions about private providers, thinking their motivation was wealth (theirs) over health (residents'). Having laid siege to and conquered the moral high ground, one morning I woke up and smelt the coffee (the 'Moral High' ground coffee, natch). As a head of inspection I was making my money out of care as well. So why was my lucre cleaner than a private provider's? Even as a head of unit, there were inspectors in London who earned more than me. So, is that right? Is that fair? I know of inspectors who pull in about £28,000 a year (and they only have four or five homes to inspect). Now, I'm pleased for anyone who can wangle such a deal but, as it's public money we're talking about, the crucial question has to be: do they deserve it, or rather, do they *earn* it? The same must be asked of private providers. If an owner pulls £75,000 a year and the home is full of happy, contented, fulfilled and spirited residents (and provided the staff are equally well cared for), then why not? Perhaps inspectors should announce on their arrival how much they earn a year so the £14,000 a year home manager can take that into account when judging the inspector's performance.

And it's clearly a myth that providers are all rolling in readies, lighting Cuban cigars with rolled-up fifties, while checking the Rolex for bank opening times. It seems that more and more providers rather than going to the bank are simply going to the wall. And anyway providers need to make money: keeping the business afloat keeps the home open. The upshot is that, perhaps side-stepping the larger companies, owners don't make as much as popularly believed. As one owner/manager said: 'You work 24 hours a day and it's extremely stressful, demands on your time are high and

To care for people and by doing so a good sense of fulfilment.

remuneration for what you do does not compensate for the effect this job can have on your health.' Long hours, demanding work, stressful (would you take the risk?): I am sure most providers do deserve and do earn it. Clearly some don't. But we could say the same about inspectors, social workers, managers in social services departments, and almost anybody else. Let's judge the many by the many, and not the few.

Many providers turn to care, as one did, 'to make a difference to people's lives both residents and staff (for the better).' As did another provider who said: 'I felt an affinity for the elderly and hoped that I could provide a home where a combination of care and stimulation would enhance all our lives.' And another who wanted 'to be in a position to ensure quality care and make a difference.'

The lure of making a difference, securing job satisfaction and owning your business ('to be my own boss') was a tempting mix for many. One provider said: 'Because I felt that I wanted to put something back into the community that was good and worthwhile. Also in the hope that someone would care for me in the way that I care for others with compassion and sensitivity if I ever needed it.'

We had a desire to serve our community and care for the elderly.

Another striking trend was the number of providers who were unhappy with standards where they were working and decided to set themselves up to show how it should be done. It seems disaffection with the way, in particular, councils run homes has become a breeding ground for owner/managers. As one provider said: 'Worked for a local authority for 15 years and felt that I could offer a better service myself.' And another: 'Previously worked for the local authority, became frustrated by the way they offered residential care and wanted to do a better job.' Again: 'Fed up with public sector.' And yet again: 'Disagreed with new manager's policies in social services run home.' And finally: 'Fed up working for someone else with lower standards!'

Clearly, poor care standards have inspired people to go out and do things better themselves. And not just because they had experienced poor care through working in residential care. For example: 'I looked for something to do and I had been disappointed in residential care offered to relatives.' However, interestingly, nobody suggested that they became a provider because they were inspired by *good* quality care.

Older people must be respected and their dignity paramount. I felt I could do this and wanted to.

Some providers were confident why they chose their careers because they are confident in their abilities. For example this council home manager: 'I know I do it well!! ' This contrasted sharply with another council home manager, whose experience had taken its toll. Asked why they became a provider they said: 'Difficult to say nine years on.' Finally, the same question brought this curious answer: 'It was suggested by registration and inspection officers.' I trust they made it a recommendation and not a requirement.

what's it like being a provider?

We asked 'what's it like being a provider?'

VERY difficult. Many different people telling you how to do your job.

A juggling act.

Juggling balls.

Being a juggler!

Challenging, stressful, satisfying, rewarding.

Hard work!!

Hard work, but can be rewarding most of the time.

Hard work, an awful lot of paperwork to be done, rewarding, time consuming, frustrating.

As will be quickly picked up from the side margin quotes, providers believe that their work is hard, demanding and stressful but ultimately rewarding. It seems they have pitched battles with below-par budgets, are bombarded with paperwork and are besieged by bureaucracy. But like seasoned campaigners they resolutely soldier on. Actually the war-like imagery is perhaps misplaced. Providers say that being a provider is like 'juggling resources with meeting needs', 'jumping through hoops', 'spinning plates' and performing 'a juggling act of budgets and provision'. It seems that an image of circus performers is more appropriate. Watch out for Billy Smart Care Homes plc.

However, the message from providers is serious. The quote at the start of the chapter says it all for many providers: they feel under fire and undervalued. One provider feels it is 'a battle between what you want to do and what you can do with financial restraints. Feel got at by all sides, clients, inspection team and company.' Another provider described their job as 'a constant struggle to achieve a balance between what is required legally, wanted by staff and residents, and expected by employer.'

The feeling that undue pressure is brought to bear by inspectors is strongly felt by some. One provider noted that 'inspectors always have to justify their visits by finding fault.' A manager of a private home who described life as a provider as 'very difficult' also picked up on this theme: 'You are constantly having to make changes within the home, not to suit the residents but to suit the inspectors.'

Inevitably, providers link inspection closely with one of their great frustrations (others of which we'll look at later in this chapter) – paperwork. One provider (whose teeth you can almost hear gnashing) noted that things now were just 'too onerous with the ever increasing burden of unnecessary and pointless paperwork.' Another provider agreed: 'A sense of frustration over bureaucratic red tape.' Yet another provider said:

> *Being a provider is rather like being caught between two worlds. One world being the resident and their daily needs, the other being the world of paperwork demanded by various agencies to 'prove' the job is being done 'properly'.*

Antagonism towards paperwork is by no means solely copyrighted to providers. We would, in all our different walks of life, prefer to fill in less bits of paper. However, few of us really mind if we know why we have to do so and can see the value or point of it all. It is something we should adopt the 'why?' approach to. Why does that have to be filled in three times? Why am I recording this same information into two different places? Why is this being recorded at all? Discover your answers and act accordingly. Some things are

Stressful at times but overall satisfying. A lot of hard work and long hours. Lack of social life.

Rewarding but difficult. Frustrating and joyful. Sad and happy.

Soul destroying at times.

Challenging, satisfying, coupled with the emotional high and lows expected from working closely with people.

Hard work – nothing glamorous in it. People do not realise how difficult a job it is and it's getting harder and tighter.

Involvement with residents' very satisfying – other areas can be very stressful.

An excellent experience in terms of impact on the development and support of individuals. However, often misunderstood in terms of intent, and without a voice.

required by law, by organisations, by inspectors, by managers and their managers. Spend time thinking about your recording systems. How can they be made more efficient while remaining effective?

A number of managers blame paperwork for keeping them away from what they came into caring to do: be with people. One manager who felt their job was both 'rewarding and frustrating' said that there was 'not enough one-to-one time with both staff and residents.' Another manager who also found her role 'frustrating', agreed: 'the over abundance of paperwork detracts from the time available for one-on-one care.' Another, who felt their job to be 'extremely stressful' said that it was 'very difficult to get job satisfaction because of constant pressure of paperwork – not enough with people.' Yet another provider said that 'as a manager I have less and less time to spend with clients – my role is that of an administrator.'

Unfortunately, and I hate to be the one to say this as I do sympathise with the sentiment, but if you want to care for residents then be a care assistant don't be a manager. Being a manager is an incredibly influential job. Other people may well be doing the caring but they will do it in your likeness. The way a home is run is so dependent on the attitude, belief and approach of the manager. Good homes will nearly always be good *because* of their managers not *in spite* of them.

Managers from all sectors were seemingly united by frustration. A manager of a council run home echoed many a providers concern over the lack of money: 'Providing quality of service on a shoestring is not easy. National recognition of the value of carers leading to better wages would attract more qualified staff and lead to better care.' While a manager of a private home who felt that being a provider was 'time consuming and hard work whilst being a challenge and a learning experience', added that it 'can also be frustrating when working for a big company as the things that need doing you have to fight for, even the basic things.'

One owner/manager said that being a provider was 'like being in a ghost train just waiting for the next blanket of cobwebs to hit you: trying not to shriek because you know all things come to an end.' It must be the fear and frustration that pumps through the veins of providers, that caused one of them to admit, somewhat sadly given the matter-of-fact comment, that 'caring is more about covering your back than caring now.'

However, to balance that view a manager of a voluntary home said simply and movingly that it was 'a privilege to be able to improve tenants quality of life.' Other providers talked about residents as if part of the family. For one, being a provider was 'like having a large family with all the individual problems this incurs.' An owner/manager said that 'my clients are part of my family not just a wage packet. Another provider described themself as 'everyone's "mother". Thought-provoker, trend setter, quality assessor.'

However, the overwhelming image given by providers of their lot is, perhaps, summed up by the following quote:

Work with and for residents – extremely satisfying.
Administration burden – overwhelming.
Financial reward – extremely poor.

how do providers view inspection?

Inspection is a positive experience and I have moved forward with it.

manager of a council run home

We asked providers which of the following statements best described the inspection process for them. They were invited to tick as many of the statements as they thought necessary. Here's what 118 providers thought.

how providers view inspection		
suggested statements	number of providers who agreed	percentage
a way of developing services	102	86%
a necessary part of the job because the law says so	87	73%
a welcoming experience	52	44%
something that happens – neither welcome nor unwelcome	42	35%
an intrusion	15	12%
a necessary evil	15	12%

Without doubt one statistic stands out the full Derby distance: 86% of providers, or in advertising parlance, almost nine out of ten providers (who expressed a preference) said that they saw inspection as a way of developing services. Almost everyone thinks that inspection can be positive for a service and help improve the quality of life for those that should matter the most. But only half of those who believe that actually welcome inspection. My maths was never that sharp, but something doesn't quite add up here.

It seems to me, at least, that these two figures might make headway toward each other if inspectors were (or seemed to be in the eyes of providers) more approachable. If this *is* the case then this seems easily mended: style, manner and approach cost nothing but time and effort to put right. In truth inspections are hard work (for both inspector and inspected) and are inevitably tense, nervous affairs, but good providers should not really be feeling that inspections are unwelcome. And good inspectors should not make inspections unwelcoming. A manager of a private home said 'I would like an inspection to be a welcoming experience but it is not necessarily the case.' A chief executive of a voluntary organisation said: 'Although a welcoming experience it is trying sometimes.'

Many providers spoke positively about inspection. For some it was a chance to talk to knowledgeable people about care and new ideas. One provider saw inspection as an 'opportunity to work as a 'team' with the Registration and Inspection Unit. A time for discussion.' While a private owner/manager felt it to be a 'chance to exchange ideas.'

Providers from all sectors thought inspection should be seen as a type of support, guidance and advice system: 'A source of information'; 'for me, an area of support in my job'. It was also seen as an external review of the quality of care provided: 'Another way we can audit our care'; 'Can be used as an audit of how you're doing.' A manager of a voluntary home thought inspection a necessary evil because 'of the imperfect world we live in and comparative recent history of diabolical standards in some homes.'

Inspection as intrusion was also a message to come from providers, with 12% feeling this to be the case. One said: 'It can be an intrusion' – the inference being that it isn't always and doesn't need to be, but can be: again, down to the manner of the inspector, perhaps? A manager of a private home felt inspection was 'an intrusion to residents perhaps but not for staff.' Another agreed: 'Personally I don't see inspection as an intrusion but I am aware that residents do.'

Unfortunately again, what comes out strongly is the way an inspection is conducted, sometimes generally, sometimes by different inspectors. For one provider inspection was seen as 'irritating because each inspector demands different standards – even when no changes in the homes or regulations.' A private owner/manager felt that things had got worse: inspection, they said, used 'to be friendly, advisory – now it's interrogation/looking for faults.' Another provider felt that all the statements describing inspection in the table above 'can apply depending on the attitude of the inspector.' This was echoed by another provider whose own view of inspection 'often depends on the inspector and their approach.'

The way to improve inspection, as far as providers are concerned, is clear. Perhaps inspectors should note that in their little black books. And if they then carry out inspections in an open, honest, approachable and supportive way, inspections will become, as one happy provider put it, 'Something not to be afraid of.'

the ideal provider

CARE HOME OWNER seeks discreet twice yearly visitor for mutual appreciation and recognition of good practice. I come highly recommended and with all units moving and handling well.

what providers think makes an ideal provider

When describing the ideal provider, providers themselves concentrated on caring qualities and the need for the provider to be a people person at heart. One provider said that all a provider needed was 'Halo and wings.' Here's what other providers had to say makes for an ideal provider.

> *The provider needs a lot of patience and understanding with both clients and staff. Tolerance also helps when dealing with the public.*

> *Person providing care to a standard they would expect for their own relatives.*

> *Someone that has also been a relative of a person being cared for in a residential or nursing home.*

Someone who persistently chases changes for the right reasons – and also perhaps recognises when to stand still and take stock.

One who can meet all claims in their brochure and is flexible enough to accommodate needs of new residents.

Must be a 'jack of all trades': crisis manager, counsellor, friend, accountant...

One who has the respect of both residents and staff and other professionals, and is open to new ideas for improving a service.

Flexible, welcoming, warm person who makes people feel important.

Someone who has the client's best interests at heart; someone who cares more about others than themselves; a carer.

Knowledgeable, caring person with an eye for business.

A conscientious, responsible, analytical person who has a genuine interest in the welfare of those in their care.

Someone who enjoys people, appreciates that the residents have to live in the home and not the owner.

A dedicated person who puts the needs of the clients above all else.

Shrewd business abilities whilst compassionate and caring.

A happy and content workforce with the residents at ease in their surroundings.

One who puts the interests of residents first, despite any 'pressure' from owners.

To provide a good quality service in which the clients, the people are listened to at all times. It doesn't have to be fancy, just homely.

what inspectors think makes the ideal provider

While I believe that inspectors should permit a healthy cynicism to run through their veins, it seems that, for some, an inflamed bleeding heart arrogance is clotting things up. The way inspectors describe the perfect provider tells us a lot about their perception of the ordinary, everyday run-of-the-mill provider. For inspectors, the perfect provider is one that listens, responds and makes changes. For that presumably read: listens (to inspectors), responds (to inspectors) and makes changes (suggested by inspectors). Out of this two compelling and worrying conclusions could be drawn: one, that providers clearly do not know what they are doing and thank the lord for inspectors who clearly do; and which leads into the second, that inspectors know best.

Undoubtedly out there in the big bad real world there are owners, managers and staff who in a small, cosy, good ideal world would not be allowed anywhere near anybody who needed care. Similarly there must be inspectors who do their employers and the profession no favours. Hell has undoubtedly manufactured both providers and inspectors. But we have to believe they are all a very small minority. It seems only right (and not unfailing optimism) to suggest that the starting point of any relationship between provider and inspector must start at mutual trust and value. The provider is doing a job that the inspector has chosen not to. So respect that. Respect that they are doing something you are not. Likewise the provider should respect that the inspector has a job to do and for now is the best person for it. Let the words and actions of one or the other prove that the trust was well founded or misplaced.

Here inspectors describe how they see an ideal provider.

> *Someone who has their own high standards and who continues to develop.*

> *Someone who has a high commitment to the values and principles of care and who tries their best to provide these.*

> *One who is committed to providing a quality service – by training staff and investing in the home.*

> *Innovative, responsive, supportive to staff in terms of training etc, investment in establishment.*

> *Good employer with their belief in providing a quality service to residents.*

> *Someone who puts the residents first! Someone who is prepared to reflect on practice, look at new ideas and make improvements and changes.*

> *Generally more motivated by caring than profit but realistic about the need for proper business management.*

> *Knowledgeable about client needs. Seeking professional partnership with inspection.*

> *A person who aims to provide the best quality of care in comfortable, safe surroundings, and who is always receptive to suggestions to further improve.*

> *The ideal provider is one who listens to service users and actions recommendations made.*

Continuing to develop services; treats management and staff as a team; prepares well for inspections; gives residents 'ownership' of the home; gives residents good time.

The ideal provider is one who ensures he provides a quality service by ensuring the users and staff's voices are heard.

A good provider:
- *understands and implements the principles laid down in* Homes Are for Living in *and* A Better Home Life
- *has good business skills*
- *understands and implements the legislation governing the running of residential care homes*
- *places value on sound recruitment and selection practice and staff development*

Focused on residents' wishes and needs. Open to constructive criticism.

One whose main interest is the welfare of the service users. One who views inspections as part of the whole caring process.

how do providers judge their success?

Providers say how they judge their success:

My residents recommend us to their friends. Happy relatives, involved and approach staff readily. Waiting list, full house!!

Feedback from clients, relatives, other professionals, staff and inspection unit.

Full occupancy, low staff turnover.

Providers use a variety of ways to judge whether they are doing a good job or not. Generally, these are feedback from residents ('Purely and simply feedback from the residents themselves') relatives and others ('Feedback from residents, families and fellow professionals') including inspection units; complaints received; the happiness of residents; occupancy levels; and their own general perceptions.

It seems that the feedback received from residents and relatives is not collected or measured in any systematic way but rather a 'thank you' here and a card there. Although one provider described this rather well as 'Residents, staff and families satisfied with service and enthusiastic about the future.' Interestingly, many homes view inspection reports as a sort of quality assurance report – somebody from outside coming in and reviewing how they are getting on. As one provider said: 'A good reputation that is fed back to you either by inspection reports or word of mouth.' Some homes, if part of a large organisation, do have external managers to carry out reviews, but for most inspection reports may well be the only written evaluation of their home they will receive.

Knowing that residents are happy is enough for many providers. One said 'seeing residents who are happy' was how they judged success. But they also recognise that having happy residents may

Bed occupancy, good inspection reports, minimal complaints, low care staff turnover, word of mouth.

Full beds.

Response of residents, reputation in local area and reasonable profit.

Review feedback, inspection reports, support committee feedback, accreditation review, user feedback, staff responses/performance.

Feedback from clients. Reports from inspection. Staff feedback.

Residents being happy and contented. Relatives being relaxed.

The outcome of the inspection report and the opinion of my residents.

Registration and Inspection. Residents are happy.

well be dependent on having happy staff. One provider said: '...by having a happy staff and atmosphere.' Another agreed: 'By the happiness in your working environment.' A nursing home manager agreed likewise, for them it was 'Happy residents. Contented staff.' And finally a manager of a voluntary home would also judge success by 'Happy, contented residents and positive feedback from residents and visitors. Happy, fulfilled staff group.'

A main indicator for providers judging their success is how full they are: 'By being full' said one; 'Remaining full' said another. This was more so, understandably, for private homes.

One provider used the 'Number of complaints' as the way to judge success. While certainly an indicator it may be a flawed one as another provider observed: 'Not many complaints or maybe the more complaints means at least you're prepared to listen!' True enough. A home that has had no complaints might on the face of it seem a 'better' home than one that has had 100 complaints. The home with 100 complaints may well be such a bad home that it's a shock that the number of complaints is so low. But it might also be a listening home and residents are not only encouraged to complain because the home sees complaints in a positive light, but also encouraged to have a say about how the home is run. The more residents are listened to, the more confident they are to continue having a say. Also the complaints recorded might be for things like lumpy custard, but have nonetheless been treated promptly, seriously and resolved. Whereas the home with no complaints might well be providing the perfect service. On the other hand, there may be such a strict, overpowering regime in place that residents are too scared to complain for fear of retribution. Statistics on their own can tell any tale you like (in much the way at elections where not only has the winner declared it a victory but so has the other eight losing candidates). Statistics are a surface under which you should scratch.

Other providers would judge their success 'by not being complacent'; 'Reaching aims and objectives especially when they seem impossible.' Others used social work-y tactics of 'Self reflection...' or 'By drawing from the residents feelings.'

However, two ways of judging success which, if I were a provider, I would like to think I would put a lot of trust in, were as follows.

> *Customer satisfaction, when clients know this is their home for life and tell you so.*

> *I feel that if I can provide the quality of life and stimulation that my grandma would like, then I am on the right track.*

the most rewarding and the most frustrating things about being a provider

The interesting thing about this part of our research is that providers had more to say about what frustrated them than what rewarded them. This is, perhaps, reflective of our society. For example, bad news is good news for newspapers. Very little positive coverage of social care appears in newspapers, whereas negative coverage appears a very lot.

I guess, in some ways, we need frustrations. I remember a social services admin worker (thankfully not working for me) who moaned incessantly that there was too much to do, taken for granted, overworked, underpaid, only a scale 3 you know, and so on. The admin worker was then given an assistant. It ruined her. It was the complaining that kept her going.

However, we will stick with the principle of putting the best things first and look at what providers say are the best things about being a provider.

most rewarding

In general, providers were rewarded most by the happiness of residents or seeing a real improvement in the quality of their lives. As a manager of a council run home poignantly said, it is 'when you see residents take back control with challenging spirit.' Or as the manager of a voluntary home said, it was seeing the 'renewed confidence and self-esteem of residents. Residents establishing their rights.' Providers also reported great satisfaction at seeing happy, contented staff who had improved their skills and knowledge. For example, one provider said: 'Seeing residents and staff develop', and another felt that 'training staff to their full potential obtaining their qualification' was the best thing about their job.

Naturally receiving positive, grateful, warm and loving feedback is always very satisfying. One provider said the best thing was hearing 'clients referring to the establishment as home.' An owner/manager said it was quite simply 'seeing our residents smile.'

For one couple one of the best things about being a provider was 'achieving our aims and objectives'. The 'our' was pointedly underlined: it quietly screamed out to me that they should be achieving **their** aims and objectives not those others suggest or dictate.

Realising that the quality of service was as good as it could be was also an important reward for providers. One said that 'to know you are providing a good service' was the best thing, while another felt that it was 'being praised about the service you provide.' However, the last provider also added that such 'praise rarely comes from inspection units – their comments are usually punitive.'

One provider, obviously suffering from the stress and frustration of it all declared the best thing about being a provider was 'holidays'. Only one provider felt that there was 'not much nowadays' that they felt rewarding in the job. However, a more uplifting answer to what a provider found most rewarding about their work was that provided by the manager of a council run home: 'when you get it right.'

Some other responses from providers were as follows.

Seeing that your clients are cared for to the best of your ability.

Seeing happy residents and happy carers.

Watching those in our care grow in independence and achieve what they can in running their own lives.

Providing a loving and secure home. The relationships formed between ourselves and our residents.

After a client makes their home with us seeing the vast improvement in their health and regaining their will to enjoy life.

By the smiles and thanks of residents and relatives.

Happy residents, staff and homes committee. Pride in the home I run.

Good working relationships with stakeholders. Smiling clients' faces.

Developing staff.

When you receive positive feedback from residents, staff, families, other agencies, etc.

Improving someone's life; seeing results.

Making people happy.

Seeing the residents happy.

Making a healthy profit.

Clients realise they have not moved into residential care to die but to live their lives as fully as possible in a different environment.

The residents' reactions to a job well done.

Happy, fulfilled residents and an enthusiastic team.

Knowing that although not perfect the home I work in is still a long way from the kind of care provided in the large institutions not that long ago.

Building up relationships and gaining trust with those residents who would otherwise be solitary and friendless.

The clients' appreciation for what you do for them

A quiet thank you from our clients or a member of their family.

When you get a thank you letter or card.

On occasions when relatives and friends of residents express their gratitude you realise how you are helping to keep people's sanity.

Knowing that you have made someone's last few years as happy and comfortable as you can, and that families can live with this afterwards.

When a resident says 'Thank you so much – you are really kind' or 'I wish I had moved in earlier'.

most frustrating

Oh well, where to start? The frustrations seem to cover seven general groups, which are listed below in (a very) rough order of (un)popularity. Inspection-related offences are more than likely top because the information was asked for as part of the research for this book – so it probably put inspection to the front of providers' minds (as if it really appeared anywhere else).

- inspection
- financial constraints
- paperwork
- staff
- demands on time
- time taken for change or things to happen
- no time to spend with residents

The following comments need no commentary.

Understanding that sometimes recommendations made by inspectors are not always practical for the kind of residents in a home. Families not always understanding relative's illness.

Financial constraints of the organisation not reflecting the philosophy of choice and independence.

Knowing that what you're doing is the best you can do, but it is not always enough...Dealing with 'red tape' situations! Too much time wasted on paperwork rather than on actual clients' care.

The paperwork attached to the needs of residents when you would rather look after them.

Lack of understanding of client need – purchasers. Lack of understanding of client group – inspection. Being a target for sometimes unfair criticism with little opportunity to respond.

The time it takes to make changes.

Providing the standard required for ever diminishing resources.

Not being able to give the clients exactly what they want/need due to lack of support or funding.

Purchasing authorities expect very high standards for very little funding.

Lack of funds.

Red tape!

Paperwork and red tape.

Paperwork and staffing.

Unrealistic bureaucracy.

The overwhelming amount of administration generated by outside agencies

When the provider is doing all his best to give good care, the registration officer comes up with a stupid idea. This is very frustrating.

*Being on call **all** the time.*

Everyone expecting the world.

Budgets! Bureaucracy!

Wrong things remembered – good things forgotten!

Unmotivated staff. Unreasonable regulations. Inspectors' comments are unnecessary at times.

Nit-picking by inspectorate.

At first, having a list of expensive changes demanded by Registration and Inspection. But refusal to increase the number on certificate to provide business to pay for it.

Not always having enough time and not having the final say on what staff you keep.

Because of paperwork and administration even with help unable to spend as much time with clients as would wish. Some jobs difficult to delegate.

Rules and regulations that are petty and frustrating and sometimes unnecessary.

Forms, continual exposure to others' (sometimes subjective) opinions about the way service works.

We are with our residents 24 hours per day, seven days a week. We know them better than most and when outside services don't listen to us, it is extremely frustrating and makes us feel very angry.

By being told how to care by those who don't, i.e. authorities.

Under-funding and feeling undervalued.

Not having enough hours in the day!

Solving staff problems.

Maintaining permanent staffing levels without using agency staff...

Paperwork, stupid rules and tin gods who look no further than their rule book.

Dealing with bureaucracy, and all the different people that tell you what you are not doing right.

Bureaucrats not having a clue.

Inspection team and relatives.

When recommendations are made by social services that in theory do not benefit my residents at all. That more emphasis is placed on 'paperwork' than the actual service you provide for residents.

Meeting the 'requirements' of a Registration and Inspection visit then having more requirements at each subsequent visit. Reports are often subjective.

Trying to get there but not quite succeeding.

We are constantly aware of the unbalance of power. We do not feel we could dispute any ruling. For example, we have capped water temp with close valves. Social services have not done this in their own homes.

Budgeting. Moving goal posts. Meet inspection unit requirements one year to find them looking for something different on the next visit.

I am reasonably happy with my staffing levels and resources. No real frustrations. Sorry.

If you honestly know you are offering the best service you can BE HAPPY, many owners don't.

Reading through these frustrations, it does help to get a feel for what it's like being a provider. As said part of the point of this book is to try and encourage greater understanding of providers for inspectors and the other way around. If one understands better what makes the other tick and what makes them tock, then it must surely help inspection run more like clockwork. The time is right.

before an inspection

chapter 4 – before an inspection

Informing residents and their families (it's their day).

By treating each day as a possible unannounced inspection.

Filling in copious pages of data regarding all aspects of the home.

Just tee it up a bit.

providers on how they prepare for an inspection

---

at a glance

this section looks at:

what happens before an inspection takes place

how inspectors and homes prepare for inspection

the things that are in place to make sure inspections run smoothly

effective use of pre-inspection questionnaires

how inspections are publicised

introduction

The title of this chapter may well draw some puzzled looks from inspectors. In my seven years' experience as head of an inspection unit and four years of training hundreds of inspectors on how to write in plain English, it is now hugely obvious to me that nothing ever happens *before* an inspection, everything happens *prior to* one. Every inspection report in the land (except the ones that my unit knocked out) has claimed that, among other things, the report was based on information received prior to the inspection. The linguist Theodore Bernstein helpfully points out the virtues of using *before* rather than *prior to* saying that not only is *before* one word less than *prior to* and, indeed, less pompous, but that you should only ever use *prior to* for *before* if you would use *posterior to* for *after*. So be short, be simple, be fore.

standards of living

London Borough of Barking & Dagenham
**Social Services
Inspection Unit**

Standards

for older people
who live in residential care

London Borough of Barking & Dagenham
**Social Services
Inspection Unit**

Standards

for people with disabilities
who live in residential care

There are, I believe, two crucial aspects upon which the effectiveness of inspection hinges: credibility and consistency. I realise that had I fleshed these two aspects beginning with 'c' out to seven, I could have sailed bumptiously on about navigating the seven c's, but even I'm not that cruel.

In *being an inspector* we looked at the importance of credibility and how an inspector can win respect through their approachability, knowledge, experience, understanding and manner. The other key to success is consistency which is dependent on a unit's preferred process. Very few things probably rankle providers more than inconsistency: this may be inconsistencies noted by providers whose homes are inspected by more than one local authority; or between inspectors in the same unit; or the same inspector's approach to different homes. 'Why am I required to put locks on bedroom doors when that council home down the road aren't made to?' is the legitimate cry. Clearly this is difficult to accept, as one provider describes that 'locally inspectors come with so many different standards that it becomes confusing. Every so often it seems we have to change to accommodate what seems to be the whim of the inspector.'

Experience has taught me that some providers will do anything to undermine an inspection report (although I must say this has been with council run services rather than independent ones): complain about the manner of the inspector; complain about mistakes and misunderstandings; complain about inconsistencies. All these tactics (and a few more one suspects) are used to deflect attention away from what has been written. So it seems that if the credibility of the inspector is firmly established along with the consistency of the inspection process, then providers will have no choice but to deal with what is actually written in the report.

So how to ensure consistency? You will need a well defined and clear inspection process including what inspectors will look for and how. In short, you need standards. When I first started working in inspection, I would inspect to a schedule that I had cobbled together from publications such as *Homes Are For Living In*. They were imposed and so vague that almost each inspection I carried out was based firmly on whim. I realised that this was not acceptable encouraging as they did a sense of me (the one and only inspector) trying to catch out providers. I remember one home for older people that was managed by a bleach-obsessed belligerent old malcontent (I am sure he has even kinder words for me) who trusted me – rightly as it turned out – about as much as you would asking Raffles to house-sit for you while you were away. One straying resident had been brought back to the home after a member of the public had alerted staff. The deputy, half-jokingly, commented that this resident was like that – very independent. The manager sneered that he would have to un-independence her then. I said nothing. I scribbled a note. I had got him, I thought. And into the report it went. I blundered along like this for months.

It was clear that we needed standards. And even clearer that I shouldn't just make them up and start inspecting against them. Another 'c' word was about to be awoken in a sleepy London borough: consultation. We basically stopped inspecting and decided to start from scratch. We asked ourselves: if we were setting up the unit now what would we do and how would we do it?

Consultation and openness were transplanted into the heart of the unit. Indeed, such was the drive behind consultation that we ended up consulting on everything – even what people and things should be called: so we ended up with inspection advisory *groups* (not panels) and lay *inspectors* (not assessors). The people were beginning to speak. The whole inspection process was consulted on. We went consultation crazy.

It took time to win people's trust. One of the first pieces of consultation I carried out (on inspection advisory panels – complete with meet-the-public information roadshows I seem to recall) resulted in less than a 5% return of consultation documents. The last consultation exercise I carried out (suggesting further improvements in the inspection process) had a 89% return. Once people realised words were not being sliced never mind minced, and that you did actually, really-truly, in point of fact, no buts about it, honestly **want** to listen to what people had to say, and that you actually, really-truly, in point of fact, no buts about it, honestly would do something about it (and would let them know what it was that you were doing), they would fall over themselves to have their say on the next thing.

A good example of listening concerned our intention to place childminder reports into libraries. Mobilised by the local branch of the National Child Minding Association a significant number of childminders objected to the plan. We listened to their concerns and then sent out a revised consultation document with a number of reassurances. About 40% still objected. There was a majority in favour (I was one of them) but I felt that such was the strength of minority voice that it would be damaging to the unit's credibility to go ahead. In the end we received full agreement that reports could be sent out from the unit or the Early Years Team (who still had responsibility for registration, development and enforcement – the unit only inspected children's day care; a split that was flawed) but not libraries – for now. We would review the decision in one year. It was a satisfactory compromise.

Consultation, if done properly (and if you believe in it, there is no other way to do it other than properly), can be expensive and exhausting. But hugely rewarding. It's tragic to think that today there's at least one Director of Social Services who has said (as part of their closed-door policy) that even if a planned consultation resulted in opposition, their preferred option would go ahead anyway. Still, social workers know best, eh?

The first standards agreed for adult residential care and children's homes following consultation were used for three years. However, it became clear that generic standards for adults were unhelpful, particularly as they were essentially standards for older people's homes. We decided that each client group (older people, learning disabilities and mental health) should have their own specific standards. We also looked at the structure of the standards and the topics covered, and we wanted the standards to encourage homes to develop services beyond minimum requirements.

We also wanted more consultation with residents (in truth, this had not really happened before). I contracted independent inspectors and advocates to visit homes and find out what residents wanted from residential care. We also arranged for a couple of residents from each home for older people to come along to a couple of social meetings so that people from other homes could meet with each other and talk about life in a home. I had this feeling that while we spouted our shining virtues of empowerment and fulfilment, perhaps all that an older person wanted was just a good night's sleep.

The standards had previously been arranged into three sections: quality of care, quality of management; and quality of environment. Importantly, we had care first and buildings last because that's how we saw the order of importance. Our new standards would remove 'environment' as a section altogether. An example of how the standards changed for people with learning disabilities is given below.

Old standards	New standards
Quality of care	
Policy	What the home is all about
Planning and review	Working out what's best for everyone
The daily life of the home	Individual people
Race, religion, culture and language	Respect
Leisure and activity	Freedom of choice
Meals and mealtimes	Being independent
Staff and residents	Things to do
Consultation	Decision making
Health and personal care	Rights
Risk management	Relationships
Visitors	Management
Residents' finances	Staff
Quality of management	Staff support and training
Central management	Records and paperwork

Performance review	Health, safety and welfare of people living and working in the home
Staffing levels	Performance review
Quality of staff	
Staff recruitment and selection	
Supervision, support and appraisal	
Staff meetings	
Staff rotas	
Training and personal development	
Home administration	
Quality of environment	
Location and design	
The building and grounds	
Safety and security	

The language simpler – each standard addressed the resident – and the structure more logical. We wanted to start with how care should start: with principles and care plans. The care plans for residents should then be compatible with the home's overall principles. The care practice should then reflect the care planning. And finally, a home should look to review its performance against its principles which is where the cycle starts again. Every piece of care practice (whether general or particular to one resident) should be able to be traced back to care plans and the home's principles.

Comparing, as an open part of the inspection process, what a home says it does against what it actually does is hugely powerful. If a home's principles (or aims and objectives, philosophy, purpose and function, call it what they will) talk about privacy – then where is the evidence that their practice matches their claims? Why is there an un-screened commode in a double room? Why are there windows in bedroom doors? Why do residents not have nets in their windows?

Another feature of these standards was that they were pitched, in general, a little higher than before. The standards were no longer just minimum requirements but were standards *expected* by the borough. This would mean that while a home might be meeting minimum standards and not be subject to enforcement, they might still receive critical inspection reports citing standards that were only partly or not met. This would, in turn, provide a powerful incentive for a provider to raise standards.

The design of the standards was also new. Each standard would consist of a standard statement which was then broken down into three or four sub-statements. Each one of these sub-statements would have a series of indicators that inspectors would look for to show that the standard was met. The standards also deliberately used inclusive language. So, instead of saying 'people with disabilities should...' we said 'you should' or 'we should'. The idea was that everybody should read them as if the standards were talking to them. This would mean that when we said 'you should be able to...' everybody would think 'yes you should', yes we should'. It attempted to help people to see people in residential care as important but ordinary members of society.

For example, standard 6 for people with disabilities who live in residential care was called **Being independent**. The standard statement said: 'Being independent isn't just about doing things for yourself. It's about being self reliant. For example, someone might not be able to cook for themselves but can tell someone else what they want, when they want it and so on. Being independent is about being in control of your life.'

Under that were three other statements about what a resident should expect to happen. One of these said: 'If you are to become more independent you will have to take risks. Taking risks is part of our everyday lives. For example, if we peel a potato we run the risk of cutting ourselves with the knife if we're not careful. A life without risk would be very dull indeed. However, staff should manage how you take risks very carefully.'

Under that were the criteria used by the inspector to judge how effective the home was in, in this example, promoting and managing risk-taking. 'Is there a risk management policy? Who knows about it? Who understands it? Who wrote it? Who was involved? Is it particular to the home? Is it workable? Who agrees with it? Is there a clear procedure to follow? Who assesses risk? How? Why? When? How do staff handle a resident refusing to take a risk? Who decides this? How do staff handle refusing to allow a resident to take a risk? Do staff feel supported? What happens when things go wrong? What has 'gone wrong' recently? Is everything recorded? In your view – is the policy any good?' And so on.

Not only were providers given a copy of the borough's standards and expectations but also a copy of the check list that inspectors would use. This meant that providers were not only clear what the borough expected and what this meant for them, but were also clear about how inspectors would judge whether standards were met or not. This helped improve the consistency of the unit's process and indicated our solid commitment to openness.

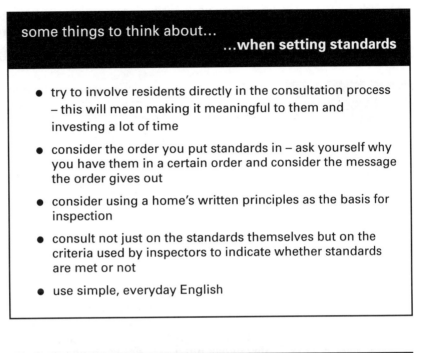

national standards

There has been much talk about the arrival of national standards. Somehow, it is believed, that the grey clouds that hover and swirl above homes and regulators will be parted by the miracle of national standards bringing brilliant sunshine into all our lives causing our minds to be blown and boggled, our awes to be inspired, our breath to be taken away and our gasts to be well and truly flabbered. National standards – the answer to all our prayers.

Frankly, I'm deeply suspicious. Well, I'm out of inspection now, so I can afford to be. I am surely not the only one to think that national standards are nothing new. What was *Home Life* if not a set of nationally recognised standards? What was *Homes Are For Living In*? Recently both *A Better Home Life* and *Creating A Home From Home* have also jumped on the national standard bandwagon. Maybe I'm just an old cynic but the wheels on that wagon look mighty loose to me.

Actually, the consultation on national standards for older people has recently been published. First impressions show that rather than exciting feelings of consistency at last, they have generated controversy. Well, there you go. Personally, I found them surprisingly better than I had feared, but then I'm neither inspector or provider. Or user.

planning and preparing

an announced inspection

If something goes well we often use the phrase 'that it all went to plan'. And usually things that do go well *are* planned. They are considered throughout and agreed. The word *plan* has been part of social and health care language for some time – most particularly in the wake of the NHS and Community Care Act 1990. We suddenly began spouting on about care plans and community care plans. However, management, in their need to breathe the air of importance, rarely have *plans*: they, god love them, have *strategies*. Nonetheless, planning became big business requiring an assistant director all to itself. And yet, like quality assurance (similarly feted by departments hell bent on being seen to act like stock market quoted businesses), planning became a complicated speciality when in realty it was (and is) a very simple concept.

If you're going in your car somewhere – you check the map to find the best way to get there: that's planning. It is simply thinking about the best way to get to where you or somebody else needs to be. An inspection is no different. Although inspectors might well inspect day in day out, most would agree that no two inspections are the same. So to help ensure a successful inspection, an inspector needs to plan for each one. As one inspector put it: 'there's a lot that goes on before the doorstep.'

We asked 30 inspectors how long they spend planning a visit. They replied as follows.

how long do inspectors spend planning for an announced visit?			
less than 1 hour	1–2 hours	3–4 hours	5–6 hours
3	21	5	1
10%	70%	16.67%	3.33%

Our research shows that, on average, inspectors will spend just short of two hours planning each announced inspection. The prospect of a 'difficult' inspection will certainly mean that more time will be needed to prepare for the inspection. Also, if the home is new to the inspector then this will affect the length of time needed to prepare.

We asked inspectors how they prepare for inspections. Thirty inspectors told us.

how do inspectors prepare for an announced inspection?	
read previous requirements and recommendations	**29**
read previous report(s)	**28**
read pre-inspection questionnaire	**27**
make brief notes	**25**
read written comments from residents, relatives and staff	**22**
talk to or meet with lay assessor(s)	**17**
plan timetable for inspection	**15**
talk to the home that they are going to inspect	**8**
make detailed notes	**5**
write part of their final report (based on pre-inspection findings)	**3**

Inspectors also said that they would:

- check files for complaints, fire officer and environmental health reports, and other relevant correspondence.
- calculate care staff hours required in accordance with number of residents and dependency levels.
- write to residents and staff.
- plan a loose framework on areas to focus on this inspection.
- talk to inspector who previously inspected home.
- analyse monthly returns of activity.
- review file in some cases – especially if inspection likely to be problematic.
- in some cases discuss with seniors if there are likely to be difficult issues.

Many inspectors are free to choose the dates of inspections. Indeed it is, as shown in chapter 2 – **being an inspector** one of the aspects of the job that many inspectors enjoy: being able to control and manage their own workload. And time like any resource needs to be managed. Planning is crucial but can be all for naught if something (as it invariably does) comes up. Inspectors who were interviewed varied in how much notice should be given, but it seems that about four weeks is the minimum and longer if possible. One inspector said that they book in report writing time at the same time they book the inspection dates. However, if the inevitable something comes up, it is the report writing time that suffers.

In keeping with what seems to be the national picture, the standard set for my old unit for informing providers about the date of their announced inspection was at least four weeks but preferably at least six weeks. And yet, in reality, we set inspection dates a year in advance. I would receive a series of dates from the contracted inspectors and my administrator and I would work out which home should fit which date. The dates always varied. We never inspected homes on or near the same date as their last inspection. Nor did we ever set unannounced dates to be around six months after the announced. It could be anytime from the next day (we did that once) onwards. We had sins, but being predictable wasn't one of them.

Homes were generally informed of their inspection date in December for the following year. So some homes got nearly a year's notice. It is possible. We always inspected homes and daycare services (adults and children) seasonally. This meant that over four years each home or daycare service would be inspected in the spring, summer, autumn and winter. It also meant that one year the gap between announced inspections might be anything between six and 18 months.

To complicate matters further we also inspected to a calendar year (which meant one 'year' being condensed from April to December to bring them into line). A complete pain to organise. But, in our view, only right, proper and fair. It was simpler for people to understand: 'we've come for your annual inspection,' we'd say. 'But you have been this year – you came five months ago.' 'Ah, no, you see that was March and this is August – it's a different year, you see.' How daft is that? I know why people do it – the precedents of tax years and council financial years but it's still daft whichever way you look at it. Also, how much more fun is a home for older people in the summer, with the residents out having lunch in the garden, than stuck indoors on a freezing, wet winter's day? I've always thought that it's a good indicator of the motivation of staff when it's clear that the processes they have are followed for the benefit of others and not for the benefit of staff. Why should our inspection unit be different?

good practice	*setting inspection dates*
	Look to vary inspection dates. Consider inspecting seasonally – seeing homes in all seasons over a four year period. Always vary the unannounced dates.

Inspectors generally agreed over what constitutes planning for an inspection: reading the file ('to refresh my memory') to check correspondence, complaints and incidents; checking the most recent report for requirements and recommendations; and analysing pre-inspection questionnaire information.

good practice	*paper and practice*
	One inspector would read the residents list sent by the home to identify which residents they would 'track' during the inspection. This would mean during the inspection reading those residents' files in detail, and tracking the care given back to the care plans.

This example of planning which residents to track has a lot to commend it as does the actual inspection tactic of tracking. We will look at this in more detail in chapter 5 – **during an inspection**.

Staff shortages at one unit meant that inspectors 'were not planning as we should – it's hurried'. Planning might only amount to reading the summary of the previous report and the list of requirements and recommendations. One unit tends to start all announced inspections at about the same time – 10am. Their policy is also to phone the home when they are on the way from the office. This unit also has two inspectors for the announced visits. They meet to discuss the roles each of them will take during the inspection: 'for example, who will stay for meals'.

good practice	*personal touch*
	One inspector described how they would send out a letter to the home booking the inspection about six to eight weeks in advance. This would then be followed by a phone call to the manager to agree the date and time. The inspector was keen on the personal contact as they felt that it 'helped set the tone for inspection'.

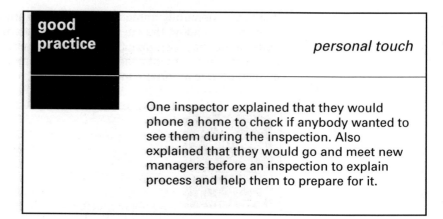

good practice   *personal touch*

One inspector explained that they would phone a home to check if anybody wanted to see them during the inspection. Also explained that they would go and meet new managers before an inspection to explain process and help them to prepare for it.

I think that this personal touch is generally the right way to go: it helps to humanise the process. One inspector said that they would only ever talk to a service if it was to be their first inspection. They did not see the need to do so after that. All communication would be by letter. A simple, quick phone call can be so effective. And even inspectors must be able to find the time to do that. Similarly a quick call to a lay assessor can be very helpful.

While most home managers would want to be present at the inspection anyway, many units require the manager to be there. 'The manager needs to be there [at an announced inspection] because the administrative review of the home is the main focus,' said one inspector. This then is also why the inspector should be keen to build up a personal rapport with the home's manager.

One inspector, honestly at least, admitted that not much time is spent reading relative or resident questionnaires as they rarely come in. The inference was that people don't really bother to write in unless there's a problem. It's safe to think that way – saves time trying to work out the real reasons why. Perhaps the questionnaires are poorly designed or do not grab the attention never mind the imagination of people.

One of the recurring themes of this book is the disappointment that a lot of inspection units do not think enough about the look of things: questionnaires, reports, publicity, posters, leaflets and so on. Yes, the content, what you say, is more important but people respond like with like. If you send out a badly photocopied, dull-looking questionnaire it will send out a message that you couldn't really be bothered to spend any time on this. And if you couldn't really be bothered why should someone else be bothered to fill it in? Something that looks like effort, thought and time have gone into it will likewise attract similar commitment. 'But we're inspectors not designers' may well be the cry. But in one sense you would be wrong. Inspection, like it or not, is part of the communication business: and how you communicate information (including the design or look of things) is integral to your job. And, anyway, you don't have to be a designer with swish desk top publishing packages to make things look good, clean and sharp. We will look more at this later in this chapter.

One inspector, whose unit was clearly more successful in getting pre-inspection comments than the previously mentioned inspector, said that they never read any residents or relatives' questionnaires until *after* the inspection. This struck me as rather bizarre. It's a similar comment to that made by inspectors who, on taking over a home new to them, say that they won't read the files or previous reports because they want to view and judge the home with an open mind. Unless the previous inspector was worse than useless then this seems to me an extraordinary line to take. I'm not sure what's at work here but might it be serious naiveté or some slightly under-controlled ego that wants to find it all out on their own and then have it all confirmed by others – proving just how fab they are at their job. A good inspector surely can collect as much pre-inspection as possible and still keep an open mind about it all – leaving judgements aside until the whole inspection experience is completed. Conversely, anecdotal evidence points to Ofsted inspectors coming to schools with pre-conceived ideas, taken from the pre-inspection information, which rarely change during the inspection. Given that so little time in a year will be spent in any one home, inspectors must surely welcome all the help they can get.

planning and preparing

an unannounced inspection

It would seem logical that since unannounced inspections are generally shorter, sharper, more focused visits then the planning and preparation would follow suit. And, that indeed, seems to be the case:

how long do inspectors spend planning for an unannounced visit?		
less than 1 hour	1–2 hours	3–4 hours
16	**13**	**1**
53.33%	43.33%	3.33%

On average inspectors spend just over one hour planning and preparing for an unannounced inspection – roughly half the time spent, on average, preparing for an announced inspection. With the unannounced inspection being essentially characterised as a follow-up visit to the announced inspection, the preparation was mainly reading the announced inspection report.

how do inspectors prepare for an unannounced inspection?	
read previous requirements and recommendations	30
read previous report(s)	25
make brief notes	25
plan timetable for inspection	14
talk to or meet with lay assessor(s)	10

One unit's approach was to have focused but more regular inspections. An inspector explained: 'All visits are based on the standards. I may visit an establishment up to 10 times a year. On these unarranged visits I may consider one or a number of standards. To prepare for these visits I may look at the part of the report of previous years which refers to these standards.' This approach has a lot to commend it. An inspector will be seen more often allowing residents and staff to get to know them. Ultimately, it may serve to lessen the anxiety for staff as they will get used to having the inspector around the place. The inspector will profit from seeing the home perform at different times and thus will be able to build up a fuller picture of the home (although still only in snapshot) than perhaps can be gauged from one announced and one unannounced visit. However, this needs to be set against slipping into an over-familiarity that could border on collusion. The arguments need to be weighed up and a balance struck. And probably a few more clichés will be needed down the road.

Presumably all the visits over the year would result in a single report. The downside here would be that a home would have to wait a considerable time to receive its report from the first visit. It may also be quite difficult for the inspector, dependent on their workload, to remember which home is which – as they must surely blur into one at some stage. This would require making detailed notes immediately after each visit. Presumably if there was cause for concern an interim report or emergency report would be submitted.

Also relying solely on unannounced visits has (as with most things associated with inspection) advantages and disadvantages. The main advantage is that you would get to see the home more like it really is. However, this may only be short-lived as once it's known that an inspector is on the premises... The main disadvantage is that residents, relatives and others do not get a chance to think about what they might want to say to an inspector. Relatives, in particular, who are a huge source of information and comment, would only get to see an inspector by chance. Leaflets can be left asking people to contact the unit. Fine. But it is unlikely that relatives will do this unless there is a problem or concern. It could also mean that inspectors, in the eyes of relatives, are seen as people to go to only when things go wrong or when there's trouble. It may only serve to help reinforce the negative image of inspection.

It is for this reason that I changed Barking & Dagenham's original inspection policy which was to inspect unannounced only. No point in telling people you're coming, I thought, you'll never get to see how things really are. But it meant that I was missing out on a lot of information from people who would know a home a lot better than I ever would. It was a policy that probably saved the unit a fortune in administrative costs (questionnaires, postage, photocopying) but wasn't the best one. My then-administrator would, undoubtedly, disagree.

And anyway, every inspector in the country will know (or at least suspect) that a home will be looking its best for the inspection, as even providers admit later on in this chapter. There's nothing wrong with that. If you have people coming over to your house for dinner or to visit, you'll tidy up, buy fresh flowers and so on. It's only natural. I remember a manager of a home for older people telling me that I was welcome anytime because she was confident that during an inspection I would see how things were: 'we might do things a little better,' she admitted, 'but we'll not be doing things any *different*.' Nothing wrong with that at all.

tooled up?

So what sort of things do inspectors take with them on inspections? Thirty inspectors told us.

what inspectors take with them on an inspection	
checklist or standards or both	28
previous reports	26
thermometer for water temperature	24
pre-inspection questionnaire	23
hand-held tape recorder	4
luxometer	1
regular camera	1
tape recorder (with external microphones)	1

One inspector said they would take some of the above but would only take a camera and portable photocopier if there were serious concerns.

No inspector admitted to taking a video recorder, thermometer for fridge or freezer temperatures or a probe to test food temperature. However, inspectors also said that they would take:

- most recent file. Wireless space measure. Tape measure. Penknife.
- green book – for contemporaneous notes (at least the colour is friendlier than the little black books in the department of health's *Briefcase*).
- Environmental Health Officer reports, complaints, incidents, fire officer report. Minor repairs checklist. Policies and procedures relating to the home.
- quality monitoring form, minor repairs checklist, feedback form, blank inspection report.
- legislation, guidance. The homes pack devised by the inspection unit.
- electronic measuring device.
- list of residents' names and next of kins; list of staff names.
- copies of fire safety reports or environmental health reports of last inspection if available.
- standards and relevant legislation.

One inspector admitted honestly to not knowing what a luxometer was. I admit only finding out they existed when I was part of the group working on revising *The London Guidelines* – a document that set standards for homes in London. The detail and prescription of these guidelines were quite intense. Thus we had a standard that lights should be at a minimum level of brightness, defined by lux. While I was wondering what a bar of soap had to do with it all, somebody (in an Emperor's New Clothes kind of way) asked how on earth would we know? How would we know if a light was meeting the minimum lux standard? Some bright spark (who I immediately took a shine to) made light work of it all and illuminated us with the answer: a luxometer, they said. Always fancying myself to be at the cutting edge, I was not about to be left in the shade, and this seemed an edge just begging to be cut. I was enlightened: I wanted my very own luxometer.

The catalogue I saw it in was aimed at environmental health officers, but was an Aladdin's cave of delights for any inspector: food probes, electronic measuring devices and the world's largest collection of thermometers. With my temperature rising, I realised that this was thermometer heaven. In an uncontrollable, dizzying rampage, I made a capital effort to empty their warehouse. I had visions of inspectors being tooled up, fully equipped, furnished, rigged and kitted out, complete with their own fetching version of Batman's utility belt. My inspectors would be able to **smell** when a fridge temperature rose to six degrees. The SAS? Wusses. My inspectors would be slicked up and armed to the teeth with gadgetry that would make Q break down and cry tears of envy. I had not just seen a catalogue, I had seen the future.

Sadly, I hadn't seen my latest budget figures and ended up with a couple of thermometers, a food probe and some wipes. But, nonetheless, I was the very proud owner of a luxometer.

I think I used it once. The battery was flat. The dream was over.

before an inspection
a provider's story

preparing for an announced inspection

Inspection, lest we forget, is (at least) a two-way process. Inspectors might 'fess up to putting in about an hour's preparation – but what of the wily old provider? We asked providers how long they take to prepare for an inspection and 110 told us.

less than 1 hour	1–4 hours	5–8 hours	9–12 hours
4	**39**	**22**	**14**
3.6%	35.5%	20%	12.7%
13–16 hours	2–3 days	3–4 days	5+ days
7	**13**	**4**	**7**
6.4%	11.8%	3.6%	6.4%

Sometimes I think it's easy for inspectors to forget (especially those who have never themselves been inspected) just how much time, effort and anxiety goes into preparing for an inspection. For 10% of providers say that they can spend three, four, five **days** or more preparing for an inspection. Compare that to the couple of hours or so that an inspector prepares. The time taken by providers can, in some cases, be directly related to the anxiety felt about an inspection coming up: the desire to get everything 'right'; the checking, the re-checking, checking the re-checking, and re-checking the checking; and then checking once more just to be on the safe side. Others clearly exude confidence in their homes and just carry on as normal. But I think it's an important thing for inspectors to appreciate: understanding the effort that has gone into their arrival at a home.

Yes, some homes will put on a performance, but it's hard to keep that up over a full day or over two or three consecutive days (as some inspections are). An inspector might smell a rat rather than the freshly cut flowers, but bearing in mind the effort and worry that goes on in the days leading up to an inspection, can only help influence a more human approach. It's fair to say that inspectors, certainly most of those interviewed as part of the case studies, do recognise the effort and worry, and do make sure that the providers know this too.

the day before

preparing for inspection

We asked providers how they prepared for inspections. Some prepare in much the same way as inspectors:

Checking last inspection report and addressing a.s.a.p.

Re-read last inspection report.

Check previous inspection reports and recommendations.

Double check that recommendations from previous visit have been addressed or are in hand.

Think about what has happened since last visit.

While a few providers are confident enough in their service to claim to do little or nothing in the form of preparation for inspection, most providers clearly do. Interestingly most concern themselves (in order of priority) with documentation, tidiness and letting people know about the inspection. I can't help thinking that this in some way reflects the importance that inspectors put on the different aspects of inspection: or, perhaps rather, what providers think that inspectors, in general, consider important. It's records, the building and people – in that order.

Because homes are run by people it is no surprise to see just how many different ways of preparing for an inspection there are. Or the different things people do and the time spent doing them. It is notable that some homes do see inspection in a very positive light and that affects positively how they prepare for an inspection. Some deliberately do little special because they respect their inspector and value their opinion of the home working normally. One provider said that 'I consider an announced inspection an opportunity to review our standards and systems of support. In addition to this, environmentally it's spring cleaning time!' Another provider said that they 'ensure that all staff and clients are aware of the impending visit. I remind them both of the purpose of the Inspection Unit (i.e. it is supportive, non-threatening).'

Despite the above positive view of the unit, this provider in choosing a word such as 'impending' betrays the fear that all providers must have (some a lot more so than others, it has to be said). It's a fear that for some is of an in-your-face intensity, for others a nagging, scratching tug around the back of the mind. Being inspected can't be easy: having someone quiz you and watch your every move and action. Even if you know that you're doing a good job, it can't be fun having someone observe you. Perhaps inspectors should imagine someone inspecting them for a day. Unnerving. During my research for this book, I accompanied an inspector on part of an inspection (a task normally delegated to my research assistant). Clearly I wasn't inspecting the inspector, even though the owner of the home believed gleefully that I was, but it was equally clear that my presence there brought extra pressure upon the inspector.

in homes we trust

Some sort out the paperwork:

I usually work with the manager the day before the inspection to make sure that all documents are all up to date.

Making sure that all relevant paperwork is readily available.

helping residents to prepare

Ensure paperwork is at hand. Return questionnaire. No other preparation needed.

The statistics asked for take a lot of research, particularly looking back at residents and staff who have left us in the previous year.

Chasing misplaced records.

Also that residents care plans have been reviewed even if I know that the care required has not changed.

Double check paper work, have a staff meeting to discuss any areas where improvements could be required.

It is notable just how much trust is placed with the home to inform and prepare residents, relatives and others. Homes are frequently asked to put up posters, hand-out leaflets and questionnaires, and talk to everyone about the inspection. I know that some units ask for a list of residents' next of kins so that they can contact them direct. This is probably better than leaving everything to the home, but can be very expensive and also may even be unlawful. The Data Protection Act requires that information can only be used for the purpose for which it was asked for: so unless each next of kin when giving the home their name and address expressly agree that it may be handed over to the inspection unit, the unit in requesting the information and the home for releasing it may both be breaking the law. Heads of inspection would be well advised to check with their legal sections or data protection officers.

Nonetheless most units rely on the home as the distribution centre for questionnaires and so on. It's healthy for units and homes to work together in this way.

It is reassuring that many providers take time and effort to speak with residents about the inspection by explaining the process, saying that residents can meet in private with the inspector if they wish and reassuring them that everything will be okay. One provider said that they prepare for an inspection by 'informing residents and their families (it's their day)', which is an excellent attitude to hold.

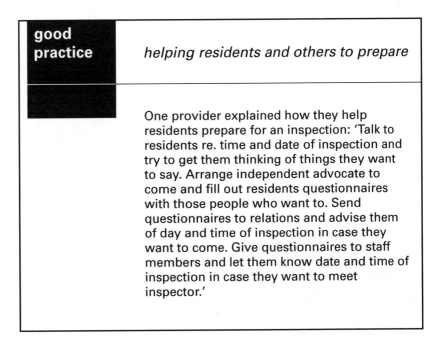

good practice   *helping residents and others to prepare*

One provider explained how they help residents prepare for an inspection: 'Talk to residents re. time and date of inspection and try to get them thinking of things they want to say. Arrange independent advocate to come and fill out residents questionnaires with those people who want to. Send questionnaires to relations and advise them of day and time of inspection in case they want to come. Give questionnaires to staff members and let them know date and time of inspection in case they want to meet inspector.'

Some inform residents, relatives and staff:

In Barking & Dagenham we thought about how we could better involve residents in homes for people with learning disabilities in the build up to an inspection. They had always been the focus during the inspection but we hadn't done much work around how to involve them before and after an inspection. After talks with the local Mencap, we contracted them to provide advocacy services to residents one week before an announced inspection and one week after.

Notify families.

An advocate would visit a home and explain to residents why there was to be an inspection and what will happen, and help them to think about what they might want to say and fill in questionnaires with them. An advocate would return a week after the inspection to check with residents how they got on, whether they had managed to speak to the inspector, and whether they had said what they wanted, and so on. It was a great success: not only did it help involve residents more in the inspection, it was also a very useful quality monitoring exercise for the unit as we would get feedback from residents on how the inspection went and what they thought of the inspector. This feedback had, until then, been largely confined to the home's response to a report.

Notices put up for residents, relatives and staff. Check systems are up to date and all easily available for inspector. Be aware of what they will want to check.

a little extra encouragement to get things done...

For some providers the 'impending' visit is obviously the jolt to get done all those things that you had intended to do, but hadn't quite got around to yet. Suddenly policies get written, repairs are made and the new filing cabinets are bought. Nothing wrong with that, I reckon. Let the inspector whose unit did not do one thing to prepare for their inspection by the Social Services Inspectorate cast the first stone. One provider seemingly hits inspection preparation overload: 'Ensure fire checks, electrical certificates, gas up to date. Fix any damage caused by residents. Check care plans up to date. Ensure cleaning rotas being done properly. Stop any ongoing improvements and remove any items to do with this: tools, slates, paint etc. Ensure gardener, window cleaner come the day before. Shampoo all carpets day before – usually some one gets the runs! Type lists of staff, including qualifications, length of service etc. Return questionnaire.' And then in the afternoon...

That all staff on duty are aware of the visit and advised to co-operate with the inspectors.

While, in stark contrast, some providers just 'try to keep the day as normal as possible.'

and then there's all the stuff the inspection unit want...

One provider summed up the feeling of many, I suspect, by saying that they prepare for an inspection by 'filling in copious pages of data regarding all aspects of the home.' Inspection units ask, it seems, for all manner of things before an inspection. One provider noted that they spend their time 'preparing requests to send to registration, i.e. rotas to cover 4 weeks; list of residents – names – funding with admission date; name and address of next of kin and phone number. List of staff – names – addresses, hours worked and date employment commenced. Providing staff names and times so that they can be interviewed.' And that wasn't it all, that was only a taster of what that particular unit expected.

Making appointments for interviews.

Tell residents they will be seen by inspector and may raise queries they wish privately.

Help residents fill in forms etc if requested.

Ascertain which children are visiting at that time and ensure that they will be able to cope with 'strangers'.

As with most other things to do with inspection there is great variation nationally as to what information is asked for beforehand. Some units have great, big questionnaires, demand copies of policies and procedures, and a whole host of other information. Others have dispensed with pre-inspection questionnaires and might only request to see any new or reviewed policy or procedure since the last inspection. Most units probably fit in somewhere in between. The main point of receiving information before an inspection is to save time during an inspection. I wonder at the value of information requested by some units and given the time spent by some homes on collecting and organising this information I have to ask: why bother?

The first pre-inspection questionnaire I devised came in at a storming 30 pages. I asked for all sorts of stuff: how many staff were aged between certain given age bands; how many residents needed help with dressing, bathing, toileting; how many residents were singly or doubly incontinent; the number of staff that had attended one training course or two or three or four or five and over during the past year; and on and on and on. It took a little while to realise that while I had all this busting information, I didn't really do anything with it. Only then did it occur to me to ask only for information that would find its way into the report. The pre-inspection questionnaire came down to four pages – and one of those was just a checklist of policies and information to be ready for inspection.

good practice	pre-inspection questionnaires
	Newcastle Joint Inspection Unit have devised a system that seems to use efficiently information received from pre-inspection questionnaires. All information received automatically becomes part of the final report.

We asked providers to tell us how long their pre-inspection questionnaires were. Out of the 101 who replied (some do not receive pre-inspection questionnaires, some did not fill in the question and some simply couldn't remember, although one provider gave two answers) they did so as follows.

is your questionnaire...	number
less than 4 pages	10
4–10 pages	51
10–15 pages	17
16–20 pages	13
21–30 pages	8
31–40 pages	2
41–50 pages	1

Some reassure people:

Explaining to staff and residents who have not experienced before what is likely to happen. Not to worry.

Thankfully, for providers at least, most units (60%) keep their questionnaires down to 10 pages or less. However, nearly 40% of providers said that they received questionnaires that were 10 pages long or more. The 11 providers who receive questionnaires of between 21 and 50 pages have my sympathy. Inspection units must surely have to justify the information they ask for. They must surely look for quality of information and not quantity.

Ensure all clients and relatives are aware when they are coming and able to talk to them in private if they wish.

I would encourage units, even those with relatively short questionnaires, to look carefully again at what is being asked of providers and ask yourself that most difficult of questions: why? Why are we asking for that? What is the purpose of it and what do we do with it? If your answer sounds like the one that is often given by a frustrated parent ('Because we do, that's why') or worse still, the answer that every inspector smirks and sneers at ('Well, we've always done it that way') then perhaps, dependent on the technology to hand, the 'delete' button or the red pen should come into play.

Try to reassure residents about the intrusion

However, just because a questionnaire is long it doesn't necessarily mean that it is complicated. It might be a very well designed and easy to fill in (perhaps a tick box approach). The 30 page monster that I first sent out had less than 50 questions: a question might take up a whole page and only require one tick. Conversely a relatively short questionnaire might ask for difficult-to-get information and take a long time to complete.

We asked providers how long it takes them to fill in a pre-inspection questionnaire? This time 104 providers replied.

time taken	number
less than 1 hour	20
1–3 hours	51
4–5 hours	13
6–7 hours	12
8–9 hours	3
10–12 hours	2
13–15 hours	3

Some get cracking around the building:

Physically checking things like dates of non-prescribed medication, spot checking tablets quantities. Getting up to date on policy and guidelines issued by organisation.

Obviously see that everywhere is tidy, etc.

Ensure office tidy/filing completed.

Ask staff for extra vigilance regarding cleaning/record keeping.

Again thankfully 68% of providers say that they are able to fill in their pre-inspection questionnaires within three hours. A mean average time would be 3 hours 8 minutes. However, nearly one in five providers say that they take between one and two days to fill in their forms (the mean average for this group would be demanding 8 hours 20 minutes).

I looked at pre-inspection questionnaires from 21 inspection units. Some are very straightforward and some ask for such detail, it's easy to see how they can take such a time to fill in. One questionnaire, although 13 pages in length, required 239 answers. I am also aware of providers who, not unusually, are keen to impress, but who photocopy the blank questionnaire, fill it all in roughly and then write it all again on the original questionnaire nice, neatly and in their bestest handwriting. This may well be their choice to do so, but it does add to the time taken to prepare. Also there are those providers, again in an attempt to present their information carefully, use portable typewriters and take aeons to line up each box with the typewriter.

Given the effort that most are required to put into providing pre-inspection information, we gave providers six comments and asked them to tick the ones that best describe what they thought of pre-inspection questionnaires. This time 107 providers told us.

what providers think of pre-inspection questionnaires		
comment	number	percentage
a good use of time as it helps make the inspection more efficient	**74**	69%
the inspector asks some of the same questions again	**51**	48%
easy to complete	**43**	40%
something you just have to do	**34**	32%
a poor use of time as it's hard to see how all the information is actually used	**17**	16%
difficult to complete	**9**	8%

Some organise the staffing:

Ensuring rotas allow for sufficient staff to be available to provide the services required for the clients and additional to answer any questions.

Arrange staff cover for manager to be available.

Make sure that we are able to meet inspectors personally.

As can be seen, pleasingly, nearly 70% of providers feel that pre-inspection questionnaires are a good use of time. Three providers were particularly positive about the usefulness of pre-inspection questionnaires. One wrote that it was a 'useful tool for the provider.' Another said that it 'helps clarify staffing situation', while a third said that it 'can also assist provider in monitoring service especially when completed with residents.'

However, an unhealthy 30% do not share the view that a pre-inspection questionnaire is all that good a thing. Interestingly, nearly half of all providers say that despite answering on the questionnaire, they are asked the same questions again by the inspector. Understandably, this may happen if the inspector is looking to clarify an answer or is looking for evidence to support it. However, all too often inspectors do simply duplicate information. This may be because checklists used by inspectors during inspections and pre-inspection questionnaires do not relate to each other in any systematic way. It may also be that while, say the checklist, has been revised this hasn't happened to the pre-inspection questionnaire.

Being asked the same question again (for no apparent good reason) must be fairly irksome for providers, particularly as the main aim of pre-inspection information is to save time during the inspection. This and the repetitiveness of being asked the same questions year in, year out also struck a dull and tiresome chord for providers. One provider said that 'much information is duplicated year after year, i.e. list of staff and qualifications, also list of staff who leave.' Another agreed: 'all information given has already been given and is asked for again for statistics.' This 'very time consuming' process for one provider is all the more soul destroying for another who talked about getting the 'same frustrating questions all the time', or what another called the 'annual repetition of permanent environment, i.e. room sizes, etc.' However, one provider did acknowledge that their inspection unit (**Kingston-upon-Thames**) is looking at how they can make sure the same questions are not asked again (or as they put it 'our inspection unit is addressing this issue').

And some just well...

I do very little preparation as I feel the inspector should see the home as it always is.

There is no pre-preparing.

I don't.

Complete questionnaire sent to us. Things just carry on as normal.

Regular monthly regulation visits minimise time spent preparing for inspection.

Other than the paperwork we do not do anything.

Ideally if all units and homes had computers, then repetition should happen less often. Indeed, one provider said that they 'have now just started to update information from computer to save time.' A home could keep a copy of their last pre-inspection questionnaire on disk and simply write over where change has occurred. The basic information would only need to be typed in once: from then on it's just a case of typing in changes. To be fair, many units have recognised that a lot of information asked for is repetitive and unlikely to change: name of home, address and so on. These units might send a copy of the previous questionnaire and ask homes something like put a n/c (for 'no change') or leave alone where the information is the same as last year and only note changes. This is a commendable approach if a tad untidy. **Solihull** send out a questionnaire in which they fill in as much as possible asking providers that 'where there is new information, or where the information stated is no longer valid, please amend accordingly.'

As ever, it's difficult to generalise but most inspection units should have the technology to rebuild their pre-inspection questionnaires. Some units may well not yet have traded in their Amstrad word processors or still cling to their Coronas while others are probably so hi-tech that the only time they will see paper is if they get their P45. Nonetheless, most units should be able to make life a lot easier for people. Apart from putting in the information for the first time it would be fairly painless for units to hold (on disks) a pre-inspection questionnaire for all homes.

This would mean that when a home receives its questionnaire, the basic information (or what one unit calls bizarrely 'Principally Static Information'), at least, is already recorded. I am somewhat obliged to recall Jasper Carrott's insurance claims sketch in which he says that you are always asked by the insurance company for your name and address – and yet they sent you the damn form. Is that a million miles away from posting out pre-inspection questionnaires to homes and asking for the name and address of a home, their registration category, numbers registered for, name of owners and so on? The question *Are the premises divided into group living? YES/NO* need never be asked again. Nor should *State whether Voluntary/Private/ Local Authority*, which, unless the inspection unit thinks that homes in its area have a habit of changing sectors without telling them, is a lazy question.

Another unit even asks homes to fill in the date of the last announced and unannounced inspection: saves them looking it up, I suppose. Indeed, one pre-inspection questionnaire I read even asked for the name of the home twice (once for a small box and once for a big box).

Solihull, Cambridgeshire and others use their pre-inspection questionnaires to ask providers for the 'statistical information on numbers of residents, admissions and discharges' required by the department of health. Although adding to the burden on providers, this is not the fault of inspection units, and to gather this information in this way seems sensible enough.

some approaches to pre-inspection information

In this short review we will look at the design and content of:
- pre-inspection questionnaires for homes
- pre-inspection questionnaires for residents, relatives and staff
- publicising an inspection

pre-inspection questionnaires for homes

If the selection I reviewed are truly indicative, then pre-inspection questionnaires are about as standardised as fingerprints. Some units, including **Liverpool** and **Bournemouth**, ask for very little (although they do ask for the name and address of the homes). Liverpool just asks for changes to the building, staff and residents since the last inspection plus a ethnic monitoring chart for staff and residents. Bournemouth does not use a pre-inspection questionnaire, preferring the home to send in items listed as required. However, they do ask for information on residents so that they can select the most dependent residents and track their care.

It was good to see that some units, including **Lancashire**, took the time on their pre-inspection questionnaires to explain what the purpose of collecting this information was.

good practice	information sent out by the unit
	Brighton and Hove have a guide for providers called 'Are you ready for your inspection?' This is an excellent idea, explaining to providers what to expect, what is required and what will happen before, during and after an inspection.

Most units who send out pre-inspection questionnaires also request items to be enclosed (brochures, terms of residence, complaints procedures, aims and objectives and so on). However, these requests are normally dotted about the form which is, of course, sent back. Some units helpfully provide a check list on separate sheet so that providers can see at a glance whether they have enclosed all items requested. Others, for example **Derbyshire**, also helpfully list the items that inspectors will want to look at on the day of inspection. Again this would be even more helpful if it was a separate item and not part of the returned questionnaire.

However, it seems that requests for documents and policies and so on to be sent to the unit might, more often than not, be duplicated also. Again, it seems sensible only to request things that have changed since the last inspection.

good practice	*information kept by the unit*
	South Tyneside Joint Inspection Unit keeps a file on each home complete with all the things requested before an inspection. This means that only changes to policies, procedures and information need be sent to the unit before an inspection.

I realise that pre-inspection questionnaires are never going to be the most exciting and innovative things, but it was striking just how tired and dull a lot of them looked. One unit's pre-inspection questionnaire was dated 1994 and, to be honest, looked it. It was typed out in courier which in the great world of typefaces is about as in touch as having Betamax. Also nearly all pre-inspection questionnaires appear to have been untouched by even basic design.

For example, one unit did not number its (126) questions and would leave the equivalent of one line of typed space for a provider to answer questions like: *How do you monitor performance of staff?* and *Do you have a Charter of Rights and Equal Opportunities policy for residents? Please have this available for inspection. How do you publicise it?* Publicise what? you may well ask: the inspection or the charter of rights or the equal opportunities policy? But we'll look at clarity of language in a moment.

The number of units that insist on leaving lines for answers rather than open space is alarming. Such tactics require people to write in the tiniest handwriting to get the information to fit the lines: such things put barriers in the way of people. It must surely be an inspection unit's job to get the information it wants as simply and as easily as possible. Give people room to breathe.

Which type of design would make it easier for you to answer: lines like this or without lines as in the example below?

_____
_____
_____
_____
_____

One unit that did prefer the open box approach marred this, in my view, as they used double lines to for each box. This gives the following effect:

NAME OF RESIDENT	AGE	DATE OF ADMISSION	PLEASE TICK IF THE HOME IS APPOINTEE FOR DSS

Given that words in capital letters (or UPPER CASE) are less easy to read, that too much bold is used, that the above example filled a full page, and that their pre-inspection questionnaire was on yellow paper, I think this must, literally, give a few providers a headache. Another unit also prefers the open box approach (but single lined boxes and white paper, praise be) and apart from the cover ask their (un-numbered) questions using lower case. The effect of this more appealing to the eye: it just seems simpler to fill in. However, the effect is lessened because every question is in **bold**. The whole point of using bold (or *italics*) is to highlight something: to make something stand out as important. If **everything** is put in bold then it, by definition, is not highlighting and nothing stands out. It's all in your face. To be effective bold must be used **sparingly**.

Given the amount of information required by some pre-inspection questionnaires, it is not surprising that they can take a lot of time to fill in. I can imagine the information required on residents and staff must be most difficult to put together if each year you are starting from scratch. For example, one unit (suggesting that providers should 'copy blank form and insert additional pages as necessary') wants to know for each resident their name, date of admission, gender, dependency ('from establishment's own dependency scale'), race, legal status, age and whether or not they are able to engage with inspector. In a large 60 bed home for older people, this must lead to wholesale resignations. Each file got out and trawled for the information required. Even something apparently simple like the age of a resident might take working out as files probably only show the date of birth so a provider has to work out for each one what age they are at time of completing the questionnaire.

Is all this stuff really needed? One provider said that they were 'not sure that all the information requested is necessary.' Indeed, another provider said, quite reasonably, that they were 'not sure why staff addresses and telephone numbers are wanted.' Madness, they call it madness. It's little wonder that providers might worry, as one did, that pre-inspection questionnaires are 'likely to contain some hidden agenda' or just feel, as another did, that the whole experience of pre-inspection questionnaires is 'tedious'.

It seems very apparent that questionnaires are ripe for review. Some units have even reviewed them out of existence. It would be hard to imagine that each unit couldn't refine or improve their questionnaires in some way. Units could look at each question for clarity to either sharpen up vague questions or simply make them clearer. If you receive questionnaires that have been filled in incorrectly or wrong enclosures are included and the right ones haven't been, it might be that the provider is a cycle short of a sluice or is being deliberately difficult. However, it is more likely that the questionnaire is not clear.

Certainly some of the things I have read have been less than clear. For example:

How many residents chose not to leave the home?

All of them or else they wouldn't be residents I guess.

Please send to Division the Staff Rotas for the four consecutive weeks prior to the Inspection and including the week of the Inspection

So do they want five weeks of rotas – the four before and the one during the inspection? Or is it the three before the inspection and the one during? Or...? Not sure why staff rotas and inspection get themselves capital letters, but, hey, they must be important or something.

How many residents are chairfast (predominately)?
Well, Mr Smith whizzes around at some speed in his electric wheelchair (predominately).

I have to say that I see it quite a lot but I do enjoy the choice of wording when asked: *are residents requiring special diets catered for?*

The cover of one pre-inspection questionnaire declares **QUESTIONNAIRE FOR COMPLETION BY MANAGER PRIOR TO ANNUAL INSPECTION**. And, yup, I'm sure you're a step ahead here, but on the same cover we are asked for the Job Title of the person completing the form.

The other type of questionable questions that appear in pre-inspection questionnaires are those so vague that it would be impossible to answer fully (requiring space for a thesis rather than a line or two); or those questions that neither side are sure what should go there, but providers won't admit they are not sure in case they look stupid and so just put down anything, and inspectors are too unsure to challenge in case they look stupid. Questions like *Describe how the Home meets the needs of individual residents?* Or similarly *What criteria do you use to ensure the residents needs can be adequately met by the services offered in your home?* Or *How are service users empowered to access Health Services independently?* Or *What community resources are available and how do you encourage residents to maintain or develop links with the local community?* The last question was given three lines to answer. Obviously.

While units commendably look to fill pre-inspection questionnaires with tick boxes or YES/NO answers, quite often they fall into a trap. In order to save space (again a commendable principle) they will group two or three questions to be answered *yes* or *no*. For example, this from a resident questionnaire (naturally all in bold):

Can you choose what time you get up in the morning, go to bed at night and where you spend the day?

YES ☐   NO ☐   SOMETIMES ☐

What if I can't choose what time I get up because the staff are so nice and bring everyone a cup of tea at 7am, but I can choose when I go to bed and only sometimes can I choose where to spend the day? The questions have been grouped because they are indicative of residents' choice but are nonetheless three distinct questions that require three distinct answers.

Questions should also be worded plainly. For example:

avoid	prefer
In the past year, how many workers have: ● commenced employment? ● ceased employment?	In the past year, how many staff have: ● started work? ● left?

Nonetheless, in general, pre-inspection questionnaires are considered effective and useful. Pleasingly, some units have reviewed their questionnaires and revised them into sharper, more focused sources of information. One inspector confessed that their unit's pre-inspection questionnaire 'was quite a hefty document that was a waste of time – but we've reduced it now' concentrating on profile of needs and staffing levels.'

Another inspector said that their pre-inspection questionnaire now focused more on social care of residents than their health care as had previously been the case. They also felt that the questionnaire helped providers focus giving 'them the opportunity to paint the picture. It is the provider's chance to say what they're doing.' Another inspector felt that the answers received from homes would result in 'making notes on things to home in on.' This seems to be the case also for **Brighton and Hove**. Their questionnaire has space in each section for comments to be made by inspectors, helping them to concentrate on the information given. Mind you, their questionnaire also says that 'all information pertains to the date of inspection' – so the plain English course I gave them had a huge impact.

It would have been good to see more questionnaires not only ask providers to write down 'any issues' (an issue, an issue, we all fall down) they want 'to address' with the inspector, but also to highlight any good, new or innovative practice that the home is proud of. This would also help show the provider that inspection is also about recognising positive practice.

some things to think about...

...for pre-inspection questionnaires

- be honest and critical of your pre-inspection questionnaire: what's needed and why, how do you use the information?

- consult with providers: are you asking for too much, too little or is about right? Anything they feel you don't need or don't ask?

- think about the design of questionnaires: make them easy to fill in.

- keep bold and italics to a minimum. Use capital letters sparingly. Destroy your underlining button.

- look at ways to prevent repetitiveness: consider including the basic information on each home on questionnaires so that homes don't have to fill these parts in (unless there is a change).

- keep questions simple and clear and ask them one at a time.

- ask homes to tell you about any practice that they feel is new, good or innovative. Be positive.

- oh, and **never** call basic information 'principally static information'.

pre-inspection questionnaires for residents, relatives and staff

It must be good practice to involve as many people in inspections and try to gather as much comment on a home as possible. It seems that most units try to involve relatives by way of poster and questionnaire. However, pre-inspection questionnaires are used less for residents and less still for staff (if they are included in the process at all).

It was interesting to find out what efforts were made on pre-inspection questionnaires for those who, unlike managers or owners, don't really **have** to fill in anything. It was also a good indicator of how serious units are about involving these people, particularly residents, and how they gear the questionnaires to them. Some have clearly spent time, effort and money in doing so. Others have tried as best they could in the circumstances, while others have seemingly put in little thought or none at all.

The glossiest questionnaire I saw was aimed at children in care and came from a unit in Northern Ireland. It is well designed and was a result of collaboration between the Children Order Implementation Group and Voice of Young People in Care. It is possibly a bit long (16 page A5) with 39 questions, but clearly shows a commitment to finding out what children in homes think about their care. It is also clearly aimed at children. This was the consideration when I wanted to improve feedback from children at inspections in Barking & Dagenham. We had very poor returns because we were asking the same old questions in the same old way. We weren't talking to young people in a way that interested them at all. So, I asked Stephen Hicks (who not only illustrated things for the unit but also as father of two children and a primary school teacher also seemed well qualified) to jazz up our questionnaire. He did. The A3 folded, 4 page questionnaire is reproduced on pages 89–91.

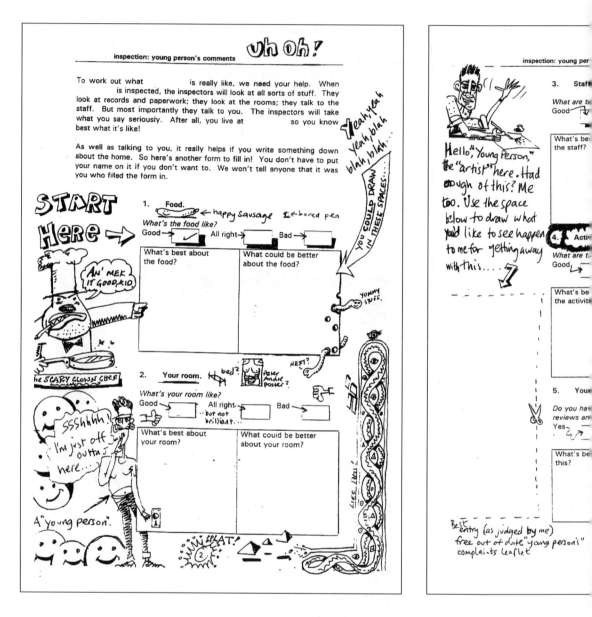

However, this caused controversy. The acting head of children's services and the acting principal officer for placements (there were only council-run children's homes in the borough) did not like it. They thought it stereotypical (the social worker image), patronising, too bitty and fuzzy (which was the point) and even drug-induced. However, as I pointed out, we were not aiming it at dull, middle-aged, speak-with-fork-tongue senior council officers, but rather at the children and young people in their care. And **they** loved it. One even wrote a letter to the unit saying that 'not only is it good, but in fact it's brilliant'. The first home we used it for had seven children and young people at the time. All seven filled it in and sent it back. Only one young person had filled in the previous questionnaire.

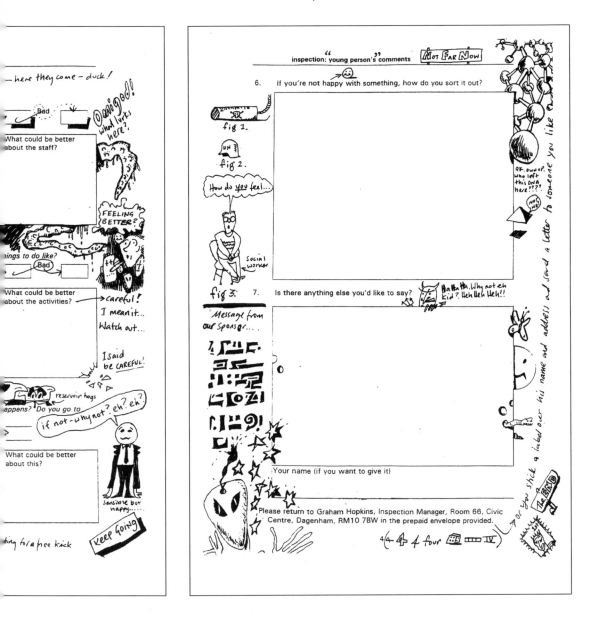

On the same principle, **Solihull** have produced an excellent questionnaire for homes for people with learning disabilities. It uses Makaton symbols as well as large printed (lower case) letters. A page of this pre-inspection questionnaire is printed overleaf.

Interestingly only one questionnaire for relatives and residents asks whether or not they have ever seen an inspection report. They all are trying to find out what people think but do not tell them what they will do with their comments (only two said that they will be included in the report) or when or where they can get a copy of the report. **Lancashire** have a basically designed leaflet for children in homes that explains inspectors ('people who visit to see if young people are

Your   home:-

	YES	NO
Is the home clean?	☐	☐
Can you go in the garden?	☐	☐
Are the staff friendly to you?	☐	☐
and to your family and friends?	☐	☐
Does the home smell nice?	☐	☐
Does the home smell bad?	☐	☐
Can you talk about what to do?	☐	☐
Can you talk about where to go?	☐	☐

being looked after properly'), what they do and reassuringly what they don't do ('inspectors do not visit to inspect young people'), but again does not make clear whether young people can read what the inspectors have to say.

It was little better for staff. Very few units use staff questionnaires. Of those that I received only the **Northern Health and Social Services Board**'s information for staff in children's homes explained that staff should be able to see a report. This appears to be an area seemingly overlooked by units. It is strange that when units bemoan (as they do) the fact that there is little uptake of reports that they do not reinforce the message to what is essentially a captive audience, never mind the wider public.

While I consider using plain English is important for pre-inspection questionnaires for homes, this must be doubly the case for residents and relatives. We really shouldn't be asking residents *how they evaluate staff support* when we mean *what do they think of the staff?* And why are we asking residents whether they have *any other issues they would like to raise* when what we want to know is if they *have anything else to say?* However, most units do appear to make efforts to make questions short and simple. For example: *Who chooses what you eat? What do you do if you do not like something?* Sometimes units send out cover letters with residents questionnaires. These letters are sometimes good and clear and sometimes pompous and jargon-filled. A good example of reassuring and friendly English for my money comes from **Stirling**, Scotland (my italics):

> *If you wish your family and friends to be involved, I would be happy to meet them also. If you do not wish to speak to me, then that is all right.*
>
> *I look forward to meeting you on...*

Experience tells us that, in general, it's difficult to get residents and relatives to take part in inspections. Questionnaire returns are often low. But perhaps units should give more thought to the design of questionnaires, what is asked and how, and make them easy to fill in. Units really shouldn't be asking residents, as one unit does, to fill in the name of the home and the date of inspection (which incidentally amounted to two of the six questions asked).

The questionnaire that looked the most interesting came from **Poole**. However, it also proves that looks aren't everything because it seemed potentially confusing (it was also in landscape which is never a good idea, I think). The question numbers were on the right (disconcerting) and they have opted for a scale scoring chart between 5 and 1 with 5 being definitely yes or always and 1 being definitely no or never. This is an effective research tool but one that I know to my cost can easily be misunderstood. I used a similar approach on my questionnaires for inspectors and providers in researching for this book. People put 5 when they mean 1 and the other way around. One person even answered some questions with a number when I wasn't asking for them. Poole should be commended for their approach to questionnaires for residents (at least it shows they have put thought into it). Maybe it's the sea air that helps clear heads down there (well their logo features a dolphin, I think), but they will always remain braver than me.

Some questionnaires were too cramped or had too much of what the unit had to say instead of leaving space for what the punters have to say. Also sadly, a number of examples I looked at were clearly suffering from years spent in photocopier hell. This may be easier for units with large turnarounds but, once again, what message is this giving? As suggested earlier, it will only say that the unit couldn't be bothered with the questionnaire. And if so, why should I be bothered to fill it in? Think about it. Long and hard.

some things to think about...

... pre-inspection questionnaires for residents, relatives and staff

- be honest and critical of your pre-inspection questionnaire: what's needed and why, how do you use the information?

- consult with people: are you asking for too much, too little or is about right? Anything they feel you don't need or don't ask? I managed to get some invaluable feedback from parents when we asked them what they thought of the questionnaires we had designed for children's daycare services.

- consider your target audience: if you have one set questionnaire for everybody then it's going to fail. Think particularly hard about how to engage children and young people, and people with learning difficulties.

- think about the design of questionnaires: make them easy to fill in. Ask yourself honestly: would you fill one in?

- keep questions simple and clear and ask them one at a time.

- keep bold and italics to a minimum. Use capital letters sparingly. Destroy your underlining button.

- oh, and **never** call basic information 'principally static information'.

publicising an inspection

I had a disappointing return on this – in numbers and quality. While some units sent me leaflets that explain the unit and inspection, I only received 10 examples of the posters that are used to publicise an inspection. A lack of resources should not necessarily spark a lack of invention, which here was sadly apparent. Most were A4 and black and white – hardly attention-grabbing. Of these, only **Conwy**'s was anywhere near approaching pleasing to look at. At least South Tyneside used red and black. Examples are set out on page 95–97.

Brighton & Hove

REGISTRATION & INSPECTION UNIT

Registration and inspection officers, inspect all homes in Brighton and Hove twice a year, to ensure that good care is provided. One inspection visit is arranged in advance and one visit is made without prior notice.

We would like to hear your views and comments on the care you have received, since you have been in the home and any suggestions you may have to improve things.

If you have a relative or friend who wishes to speak to us, we would be pleased to hear their views.

The inspector is *** who will be visiting on *** .The owner / manager will be able to inform you of the time *** will start to see residents.

If you are unable to be present, but do wish to speak to *** , please contact the unit.

BRIGHTON & HOVE COUNCIL
REGISTRATION & INSPECTION UNIT
HOVE PARK MANSIONS
HOVE PARK VILLAS
HOVE   BN3 6HW
TEL; 01273 296050 / 1

CONWY SOCIAL SERVICES
REGISTRATION & INSPECTION UNIT

WILL BE VISITING YOUR HOME ON

****

We would welcome the opportunity to have
a chat with you and your relatives during
our visit and look forward to meeting you.

If you are a resident, relative, or a friend
of a resident, we would welcome your views
about this home. You may speak to us at the
home on the date above, or you can put your
comments in writing.

WE CAN BE CONTACTED AT THE ADDRESS BELOW -

REGISTRATION & INSPECTION UNIT
2nd FLOOR, VICTORIA CENTRE
MOSTYN STREET
LLANDUDNO LL30 2RP

TEL: & FAX: 01492 574053

THE INSPECTING OFFICER FOR THIS INSPECTION WILL BE

****

Northampton
County Counc
Social Services

Is Registered

Northampton

The Annual Insp

«Inspec

The Inspectors w
com
Residents, the

In
9 C
N

Tel:

Dear Residents, Staff, and Visitors

I WILL BE VISITING THE HOME ON FROM AND WOULD LIKE TO MEET YOU.

THE HOME IS INSPECTED EACH YEAR AND YOUR VIEWS WOULD BE VALUED AS PART OF THE INSPECTION PROCESS. A VOLUNTEER LAY ASSESSOR MAY ALSO VISIT ON THAT DAY.

I LOOK FORWARD TO MEETING YOU ON THE DAY

Registration and Inspection Officer

My contact address is:-

North Yorkshire County Council, Social Services Directorate, Registration and Inspection Unit, Ryedale House, Old Malton, Malton, North Yorkshire. YO17 0HH. TEL: 01653 600666

However, streets ahead examples, in my view, come from
Newcastle-upon-Tyne and good ol' **Barking & Dagenham**.
Newcastle's poster is A3 and uses a light blue and purple as well as
black and white. Barking & Dagenham use what I thought at first was
a garish, clashing red and yellow, but hey, it grew on me, was well
liked and worked. These examples are on pages 98 and 99.

THE JOINT INSPECTION UNIT

Are visiting _____

On _____ **At** _____

We would like to hear your comments about the Home

RESIDENTS, RELATIVES, FRIENDS & STAFF
**- Please make an appointment through matron or manager,
or privately by telephoning us on Tyneside**

222 0344

NEWCASTLE
JOINT
INSPECTION UNIT

SOCIAL SERVICES / HEALTH AUTHORITY

NEWCASTLE & NORTH TYNESIDE
HEALTH
AUTHORITY

City of
Newcastle
Upon Tyne

Our Annual Inspection

is to take place on

our inspector will be

Our inspectors invite you to meet with them to have your say about the services we provide. They welcome comments about what's good as well as what you think could be better.

If you're not able to be here during the inspection - there is a questionnaire which you are welcome to fill in. There's a prepaid envelope which allows you to post your comments back to the inspectors direct.

If you haven't already got a questionnaire, please ask a member of staff. Or telephone the Inspection Unit on 0181 252 8089. Thank you.

BARKING & DAGENHAM
Social Services Inspection Unit

It is also notable that the posters from **Suffolk**, **North Yorkshire** and **Barking & Dagenham** do not give the unit top billing. The first two prefer to address their poster to residents, relatives and staff, whereas I preferred to title the poster 'Our inspection'. Again, the message here was one of inclusiveness. The residents, staff and visitors would see this up on the wall and think of the inspection as theirs, not one necessarily imposed upon them. Also the Barking & Dagenham poster was sent in A4 and A3 sizes to help fit in with whatever the home felt appropriate. A number of larger homes would ask for more copies. One resident asked for four copies to put on her bed and told everyone who would listen (and many more who wouldn't) that she now had a four poster bed. Well, I laughed.

some things to think about...

...publicising inspections

- be honest and critical of your publicity.

- consult with people: what do they think might work?

- think about the design – does it attention-grab?

- say as least as possible: less **is** more (if you want to explain the whole process do so in a leaflet and leave them under the poster).

- use colour or a bold image.

- put residents and relatives first, relegate the unit to last.

- oh, and **never** call basic information 'principally static information'.

during an inspection

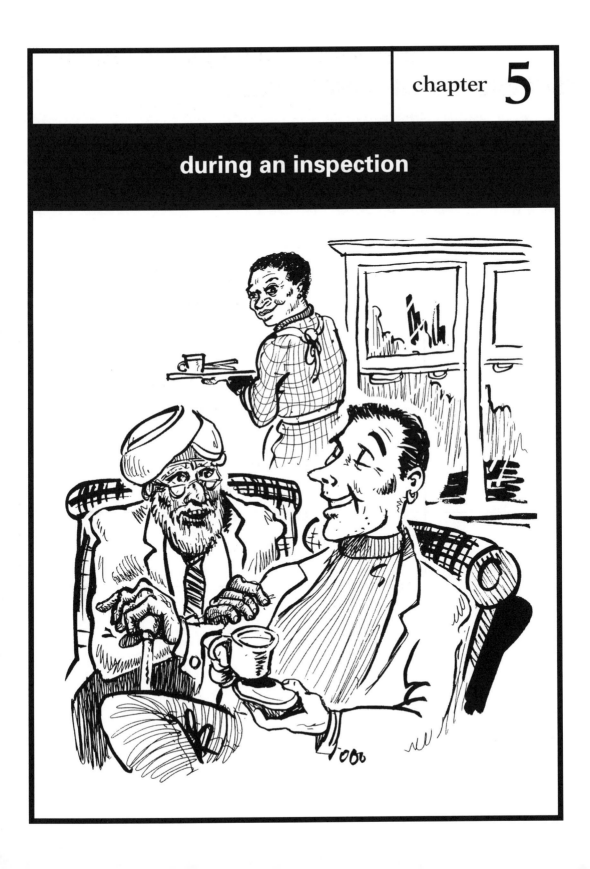

chapter 5 – during an inspection

*Although I know that inspectors won't find
anything seriously wrong, I don't relax until the
inspection is over*

manager of a private home

---

at a glance

this section looks at:

what happens during an inspection

different methods and styles of

inspection

how to involve residents

the use of lay assessors

the effectiveness of inspection

five case studies

introduction

In their inspections, and Joint Reviews with the Audit Commission, the Social Services Inspectorate (SSI) always start with an interview with the most important person or people: a director of social services, a chief executive, a chair of social services committee and so on. Being civil servants and, therefore, instinctively hierarchical, it is only natural that they would talk to the people at the top first.

There is no published guidance on how to conduct an inspection (partly the reason why this book has been written). As said earlier, it always has and probably always will amaze me how, in general terms, although working to the same laws, regulations and guidance, no two inspection units seem to do things the same way. And then, help us all, I research into how inspectors actually inspect (where there is not a whisper about how it should, could or might be done) and there is such a consistency of approach that it borders on the stuff of conspiracy theory.

Almost to an inspector, your friendly local social care regulator (naturally after polite preliminaries at the door) will either march straight, purposefully stride or quietly shuffle into the manager's office, take a seat, take up the offer of a hot beverage, take a file out of their bag and take stock. This disappearing into the manager's office malarkey fascinates me. It's clearly the unconscious equivalent of the Social Services Inspectorate's preferred approach: talk to the most important person first.

Now here's the rub. Ask any inspector who they consider to be the most important people in a home and they will tell you (sometimes even without the aid of thought) that the residents are.

Inspectors might argue that the preliminary chat or interview with the manager or owner is a professional courtesy and, after all, they manage or own the place. But, again, ask an inspector whose home is it and they will deliver the text-book answer ('why, the residents, of course') without so much as a flinch; never mind a by your leave. Which moves to suggest that they might actually believe it. So, if they do, why do they not show and prove it? One provider, in suggesting how to improve inspections said: 'spend more time with other members of staff and residents and their families. In my experience the majority of time is spent with the manager. More observation of interactions between staff and residents and cross-referencing of documents inspected.' Another said that their 'current inspection format is not helpful. It measures too many things to do with fabric and fitting of the building. Legislation needs to be written into standards that have their outcomes from a resident's perspective. This then would help to measure more of the quality of life issues the current format misses.'

In this section we will see that, on average, about one-third of an inspection is spent with the manager or owner, and nearly a second third is spent on records and paperwork (which more often than not will be with the manager or owner). This means that about 65% of an inspection is spent in that office. The office has become the inspector's home for the day.

I am fond of thinking, I really am. As a head of unit I would devote hunks of the day to its practice. One thing I often thought about was messages and signals: in the sense of *what message or signal might doing such and such send out?* For example, I wrote, designed and sent out our inspection unit's application packs for inspectors: intending to send out a signal that the unit acted independently of the department. I collected all such thoughts and put them in my messages book which I kept in my signal box. I often thought about how inspectors should inspect and the signals that certain approaches and methods might send out. Believing (as I did and still do) that inspectors only inspect because of the residents, we needed to think about how our inspection practice and process reflected that belief.

As I always say to social and health care staff on my writing courses: you must try to put yourself in the shoes of your target audience. It's also a good starting point for thinking about the inspection process (admittedly you wouldn't want to imagine too graphically what it must be like to wear zip-up slippers, but you get the picture). I am a resident in a home and I know that the inspector's coming because not only have I been told and been given an incomprehensible questionnaire to use as a coaster for my mug of tea, but because the home is awash with flowers – fresh ones, an' all. The inspection is due to start at 9.30am. I see the inspector arrive and, oh, she's gone into the manager's office. Well I guess they have important things to discuss. I suppose I will get my chance later…

Okay, maybe the tone was a bit flippant but the message is deadly serious: the manager is important: I'm not. And then what happens? About five hours later the inspector shows their face to us all being introduced by the manager or a senior member of staff, who then accompanies the inspector around the building on a *meet the people* tour. Again, what message is that sending out? For me it signals loud and clear that the inspector and the manager are in this together: that the inspector is actually part of the home's management team. If, for any reason, there are things that worry me and I do not feel able to talk to the staff at the home, I am now not likely either to empty my heart to this inspector.

Surely, if the inspector does not spend a lot of time at the start of the inspection with the residents, then they should at least tour the building introducing themself to everybody and saying that they will pop around later (saying what time) to speak to residents if that's all right with them. Also if the inspection unit was clear with owners and managers that this is their process, then they won't run the risk of offending them by not supping tea with them from the off (or is it coffee in the mornings? I must check my big picture book of social work etiquette).

It must, however, be best practice to spend the start of an inspection with residents. And then, throughout the day, go back and see people again and again. If at all possible find out if a resident is willing and able to give you a tour of the building: they will show you off. Other residents will see you with one of them and that is a very powerful and positive message. They will see your face more often, feel more relaxed in your presence, and have more time to think or remember what they might want to say. It also helps break up the monotony of sitting in an office asking questions and staring at paper. Clearly to be able to do this effectively (especially in larger homes) the percentages of times given to certain tasks would need on the evidence of our research to be overhauled dramatically. But we will look at this later. First up, we'll look at some basics: how long does or should an inspection last and how is that time organised and used?

how long is an inspection?

How long is an inspection? Might as well ask how long a piece of string is. It is certainly a question that will be met with 'well, it's difficult to say' or 'depends, really' type of answer. And, of course, given the nature of inspection work things may happen which may mean that the inspection time is cut or lengthened. And, of course, supposedly *good* homes will take less time to inspect than supposedly *bad* ones. And, of course, large homes will take longer than small ones. And so on. Of course. However, all of this suggests that we have an idea of how long an inspection *ought* to take. We may not run inspections like clockwork, but we should know what makes them tick. And this tells us how long we think is needed for an inspection visit to be credible.

How many people would consider an unannounced inspection lasting 15 minutes to be adequate? And yet they happen. How many people would consider an inspection lasting a whole week to be over-the-top? And yet they happen. I agree with a provider where I worked who said that an inspection should take as long as it needs, but that there should be a widely understood and agreed minimum time expected. I wrote this into the contracts I had for inspectors. Originally, an announced inspection would last two days (a day being **at least** seven hours long) – so over two days inspectors would spend **at least** 14 hours in a home. Unannounced inspections were over **at least** half a day – four hours. Later on, announced inspections took place over one day, and were supplemented with two unannounced visits. Some inspectors thought that they had 'got all they needed' in less time than was allocated. Thinking this reflected their efficiency, they were soon put right and told to use any time 'left' talking some more to residents.

The idea of having a known minimum time for inspections is, I believe, a good one. I am sure there are some inspectors and some providers who are happy to get the whole sordid business out of the way as quickly as possible. But equally there are some inspectors who will feel like cheats and some providers who will feel cheated not to have given or received an adequate amount of time upon which to base safe judgements and sound reports. And let us not forget that providers do also pay for the privilege of being inspected – it may well be an amount that fails to cover the cost of inspection, but, nonetheless, they do pay. So, they should at least get their money's worth.

We asked providers how long their announced inspections actually last, and 114 told us.

how long do announced inspections last?									
less than 3 hours	3–5 hours	6–7 hours	8–9 hours	10–11 hours	12–13 hours	14–15 hours	24 hours	2 days	3 days
1	23	48	19	9	2	3	1	5	3
0.9%	20.3%	42.1%	16.7%	7.9%	1.7%	2.6%	0.9%	4.4%	2.6%

It is clear that, from these findings, very short and very long inspections are a minority. Of course, in some cases inspections are carried out in teams of two or sometimes even more. So, a visit that lasts four inspection hours actually takes up eight inspector hours. Nonetheless, the average time taken for an announced inspection is about 7 hours 40 minutes.

We asked providers how long an unannounced inspection lasts. This time 118 replied.

how long do *un*announced inspections last?					
less than 1 hour	1–2 hours	3–4 hours	5–6 hours	7–8 hours	2 days
2	24	52	31	8	1
1.7%	20.3%	44.1%	26.3%	6.8%	0.8%

The findings clearly reflect national practice of using unannounced visits as shorter, more sharply focused inspections. However, it is concerning that 22% of unannounced inspections are done and dusted within two hours. Perhaps heavy workloads compel inspection units to carry out such short visits in order to meet their legally required targets, but this must surely have potential to limit their value. Meeting targets is one thing but the quality can become slave to the quantity. However, on a healthier note, the average time for an unannounced inspection would be a few minutes short of four hours.

A care home is working 24 hours a day, 365 days a year: that's 8,760 hours a year (8,784 during a leap year). Of those, on average, an inspector is around to observe less than $11\frac{3}{4}$ of those hours. That's just 0.13% of the time – so it needs to be time well spent. We'll look next at how inspectors do spend that time.

case studies

Throughout this chapter we will look at how the inspectors of the five inspection units, who were part of our case studies, carry out that mythical average, typical, run-of-the-mill, common or garden, par for the course, ordinary, standard, stock, set, everyday inspection. They are in alphabetical order.

case study, number 1

an inspector calls in...
Bournemouth

It was good to see that the registration and inspection unit's code of conduct includes requirements that during inspections its staff will 'be courteous and polite at all times' and will 'involve residents...by seeking their views about living in the home.' The unit seemed to be a strong, cohesive team with an excellent mix of experience and backgrounds. Inspectors felt valued and were very supportive of the unit's management.

Inspectors were aware that some providers would be 'more on edge than others' and would take the introductory period to reassure and explain. As one inspector said: 'I explain the process to staff – what I am doing here. I don't want them to think that there's a hidden agenda.' Inspectors use checklists to inspect against. However, they differed in their note-taking approach: one inspector said they preferred a shorthand notebook as it was 'less obtrusive', while another openly declared their preference for a clipboard (but now discarded).

After introductions and showing ID badges, time is spent having what one called a 'quiet chat with the owner or person in charge' establishing a 'professional friendliness' in order to gain 'their confidence'. Inspectors also looked at trying to 'cause as least disruption to the home as possible.' Time with the manager or owner is also used to find out if there are any residents who don't or wouldn't want to see the inspector. This may be in case a resident was ill or in bed and unable to see the inspector.

Interviewing the manager or owner and checking records generally comes next – usually starting with an assessment of care needs of the residents. Care records are cross-related with case files and diaries. One inspector preferred to inspect the records alone, others combined this with interviewing the manager or owner. This would then be followed by a tour of the building – usually with the manager or owner, although one preferred a member of staff do this as it gave a 'chance to chat'. However, one inspector said that on unannounced visits, they would tour the building first as the message 'the inspector's here!' would quickly circle the building resulting in wedges being kicked from doors and so on.

In keeping with their code of conduct, Bournemouth's inspectors do involve residents. One inspector was surprised to learn on their arrival that a couple of previous inspectors simply didn't talk to residents. Inspectors felt that they would spend, dependent on the size of home, at least 'a good half hour' with residents. Inspection techniques would include 'active listening and empathy,' said one inspector, adding that 'it must be awful to live in a home – they've lost their home, garden, pets, independence, good health, and are living with people they didn't choose to be with.' Another inspector said that they would be 'assessing smell, cobwebs, grime, looking into people's eyes.'

On accompanying an inspector on an inspection, they decided to amend their usual routine and chose (as this book suggests) to make residents the first port of call. So happy were the residents to chat with the inspector that the time allocated for the inspection over-ran and the inspector had to arrange to come back another time to finish it. This changed routine had decreased the efficiency of the inspection (as it took longer) but would have built a strong rapport between inspector and residents and undoubtedly this can only lead to greater effectiveness.

Another inspector, keen to engage with residents, told the following story about asking residents if it was okay to have a look at their rooms. 'I was told to "fuck off" by a resident once. The member of staff was mortified and kept apologising. But I said not to worry, because it shows that he has his own space.' This also shows the excellent attitude of the inspector.

All inspections are concluded with a feedback session – 'so there's no surprises'.

some thoughts on the
good stuff

openness, friendliness and politeness of approach

importance of involving residents

excellent attitude towards residents

cross-relating care records with case files and diaries
reassuring and explaining

good team spirit and strong, respected management

feedback at the end of inspection

and just
some thoughts

can more time be allocated to residents?

think about the importance attached to the order in
which things are inspected and what time should be allocated

think of ways to include residents in the feedback
session at the end of the inspection

how do inspectors divide up their time during an inspection?

It is, of course, nonsense to try and be prescriptive about how an inspector should spend their time during an inspection. But it would be equally nonsensical to say that there shouldn't be a guide. An inspector has to satisfy themself that a home is meeting the standards required or expected by the council (ultimately can it continue to trade?). An inspector needs to make judgements to that effect. And to ensure that safe judgements are made an inspector needs to build up evidence to help form and support that judgement. How an inspector collects this evidence is down to how they spend their time during an inspection.

Sadly, in my view, many units discourage inspectors from making judgements, preferring bland non-committal statements such as 'the home's records were satisfactory'. That's as lively as it gets. They fear saying anything positive in case in nine years' time enforcement action is necessary. And my, how silly and incompetent they will look then. As a head of unit I was very clear to inspectors: I was (well, the council was, but I'm sure you know what I mean) paying them to make judgements. I want to know first as a head of unit and second as an interested member of the public, what you *think about* a home. Is it any good? But crucially: *why?*

I would encourage inspectors to state their opinions, but when they did so, clearly show that is their opinion and show the evidence upon which that opinion is based. If you want reports to have an effect or even to be read, you've got to make 'em readable. We will look at inspection reports in part six but an inspector who's clear about what is expected from a report will tailor their approach during the inspection. If a reporting format is based around conforming to legal minimum requirements (a style of inspection born unto the tick box) an inspector will inevitably spend nearly all their time with things (records, policies, procedures and property) and the manager. If it's about the quality of life experienced in the home then the inspector *should* spend their time with people (residents, relatives, visitors, advocates, staff). I place *should* in italics because I fear it is not necessarily the case.

I might as well warn you now that I am about to embark on a rambling digression (just for a change) but if you stick with it hopefully the purpose will emerge. So, hiking boots firmly laced up, here goes...

I remember in the early 1990s inspecting a council-run home for older people. The manager (as they all were) was troubled, and quite rightly, by the limited number of staff hours especially given the increasing dependency of residents. Given their number of residents, had this home been required to register it would have needed to almost double its staffing. Clearly this wasn't going to happen although the council had commendably begun a programme of upgrading its homes which would result in its 60 bed homes all becoming 40 bed homes while maintaining and, in some cases, improving the staffing levels – bringing them very minimally up to registration standard (there in physic but not spirit).

The upshot for the manager was that there wasn't enough hours in the day for the home to do all that they would like. The physical task of caring had captured the staff's time. A resident being taken to the shops by a member of staff was a luxury very rarely afforded. Something that I had seen (and had indeed saw regularly) suddenly started to puzzle me: 'why do your care staff make beds?' I asked in my well-practised very simple way. 'I mean if they have no time, why are they making beds – why don't the support staff do that?'. Clearly if the member of staff was helping a resident make their own bed I could see the value. But this was a staff-only exercise and one that was carried out with a precision the military would have saluted.

Knowing full well that I wouldn't accept the 'Well, they always have' line of argument, we both pondered this seemingly imponderable question. Pondering away, suddenly the three lemons came up: 'People can see that the beds have been made. You can see that the job's been done: it proves they are doing their job.' Its proof that sitting down for a half hour chat with a resident simply cannot show. It also made me recall a deputy manager who many years previously as a care assistant was talking to a resident when the manager interrupted enquiring whether she had any work to do or not.

The point of all this is that I think inspectors suffer from the same unease: that somehow having a chat is not really what they are being paid to do. It might be extremely interesting to hear an older person reminisce about the air raids but (and especially if this will be the fourth time you've heard it in the last 15 minutes) how does it tell you whether the poor love feels empowered to ensure her cultural needs are being adequately met within a valuing diversity framework?

Similarly if inspectors are brow-beaten into being timid opinion-less creatures who strive for the ideal of objectivity, time spent with residents is clearly unproductive, unhelpful and, frankly, dangerous. It's easier, isn't it, to write with confidence that the last fire drill took place on 8 August 1999, because the records show that: it's there in black and white – it's provable, undeniable and safe (unless, of course, the records were forged but I wouldn't want to plant that seed of doubt in our inspector's mind – might set them back years). However, whether the staff and residents got on with each other and the success with which they communicated with each other is much more, hush, whisper it, *subjective*. While I don't dismiss the importance of fire drills and the recording thereof, m'lud, what really tells an inspector more about the *quality* of a home? Go on, answer honestly, cross your heart and hope to die.

An inspector has, as we have seen, on average about seven hours or so to collect enough evidence to judge whether a home is performing well, satisfactorily or poorly. We asked providers to tell us how inspectors prefer to work whether they timetable all their tasks in or just let the inspection happen. We gave them four statements and asked them to choose the one that best described their experience. A couple of providers ticked more than one box, so we have 121 replies.

how do inspectors organise their time?		
statement	number	percentage
work to a pre-arranged timetable	14	12.2%
work out a timetable on the day	22	19.1%
just let inspection happen	39	33.9%
some parts arranged, some parts just happen	46	40%

Once again there is variety between how inspection units (or at least inspectors) prefer to organise their time. Roughly the same number of inspectors prefer to have some written timetable as those that just turn prepared to go with the flow, stream or tide.

Unsurprisingly, most inspectors prefer to mix these two styles of inspection. As one provider explained: 'the arranged visit is used primarily to meet all residents and to observe practice. During the day, time is arranged to meet with the staff. This may be on the day of the arranged visit or at another date.' Clearly, if a resident or relative (or anyone else for that matter) has asked to see the inspector at a certain time, then this will need to be booked in. This would also be the case if the inspector is to take part in an event (a meal, social occasion, residents' meeting or staff meeting). However, I have always thought that apart from having an idea of what needs to be done and in what order, an inspector should let things happen around them rather than the other way around. We asked providers what they thought about this: should the home fit in around the inspection or the inspection fit in around the home? We asked providers to answer the question for announced and unannounced inspections separately. This time 115 providers answered both questions.

we asked providers which of the following statements did they most agree with:		
	announced inspection	unannounced inspection
in the main, an inspection should fit in with the service	**104** 90.4%	**106** 92.2%
in the main, a service should fit in with an inspection	**11** 9.6%	**9** 7.8%

Again, unsurprisingly, providers feel very strongly that the inspection should fit in around the home. Although an important part of the day, inspection is just another thing to contend with in the life of the home. They were caring for residents and running the home before the inspector turns up and (emergency closure procedures not withstanding) will continue to do so once the inspector has left. Sure, there will be things that an inspector will have to do (interview staff, manager) that will interrupt the normal working day. But most homes will put on an extra member of staff so that all care duties can be covered. Inspections are an intrusion but a skilful inspector and a co-operative staff team can soften the intrusion. This is why good and respectful relationships built between providers and inspectors are so important.

It is not the job of the inspector necessarily to win friends but they must be able to influence people. Thus the manner, approach and method of an inspection, as highlighted in previous chapters, is crucial. As one provider pointed out: 'I have found that their initial approach is very off-hand – as if they come to find fault – once they have got to know us the relationship improves…There needs to be an approach of working together – not against one another.' Working together is an important ingredient in the inspection mix. One manager, clearly overcooked by their experience, said, quite fairly, that 'it does not help to intimidate staff when visiting the unit.' If you just can't get empathy for love nor money, then at least substitute sympathy and understanding. This, for one provider, was a recommendation for improving inspection, that inspectors should understand 'that most providers have their service users' best interests at heart.'

So, with all the ingredients for a good inspection marinated and tipped into a bowl, the inspector armed with an imaginary whisk or magi-mix (delete as applicable to the leafiness of your patch), takes this food for thought and prepares to blend in with the home and stand the heat from the kitchen. But how does an inspector cut the cake up? Who or what gets the largest slice of inspector time and, perhaps more pointedly, who or what **should** get the bigger slices?

We asked inspectors and providers how much time inspectors spent on different activities during an inspection. And then asked them to say what amount of time they thought should be spent on these activities. As inspections vary in length, we asked everyone to suggest percentages of time rather than hours or minutes.

during an *announced* inspection, roughly what percentage *is* spent doing the following tasks? Also, what percentage do you think *should* be spent?		
task	% of time **actually** spent	% of time you feel **should** be spent
talking to residents	14	21
talking to relatives (including advocates and other representatives)	5	9
interviewing the manager (or person in charge on day of inspection) or owner	30	24
interviewing care staff	6	9
interviewing support staff	2	5
inspecting records and administration	28	19
inspecting the premises	11	9
inspecting catering	4	4

This was difficult for inspectors to answer. Not just because inspections do vary in approach, length and so on and it's difficult to generalise, but because, I suggest, inspectors and heads of units don't think about these things. An inspection is just a kind of done sort of thing. I was talking about this book with a head of unit whom I'd met at a social occasion and who looked quizzically at me (which to be fair may well have been their permanent expression) and said 'I'd never thought about that. How long should inspectors spend with residents?'

It was remarkable the number of inspectors who said that they either didn't talk to residents at all or that it only made up a small part of the inspection. Indeed the percentage given of time spent is somewhat inflated because of three or four inspectors who gave a high percentage (between 50 and 85%) to the time spent with residents. The two main reasons given for inspectors not talking to residents were that residents were the focus of the unannounced visit – the announced inspection being administrative-based; and that lay assessors were being deployed to carry out this task as a replacement rather than supplement to the inspector.

As with the replies from providers below, this has thrown up some interesting stuff. Inspectors think that they should spend 50% more time than they actually do talking to residents. At least inspectors are big enough to admit this. Being aware of what needs to improve is always a crucial battle to win. Inspectors also felt that less time than the current 58% of an inspection should be spent with the manager or owner and with inspecting paperwork. Although they still feel that it needs to make up 43% of an inspection. My own view is that that figure is still too high and that, generally speaking, 25% should be more than adequate.

Interestingly, inspectors admit that more time is spent looking at a building than talking to staff. This, for me, is troubling. Admittedly, a building can tell you things, but given a choice between inspecting a door frame and talking to a member of staff – I know where my time would be better spent. It was quite a revelation to me that very little time, and quite often none at all, is spent with care staff. And that support staff are virtually ignored. I sincerely hope that that sinister miscreant called snobbery is not at work here: *I will only interview the owner and manager and may be a senior (if I have to) but what could low-grade staff tell me?* Care staff will spend more time in any one home in a few weeks than an inspector will in a lifetime of inspection. They really know the home. As do the support staff: the cleaners, the laundry workers, the kitchen staff. To leave them out of the inspection process isn't only, in my view, seriously flawed practice, but is potentially divisive, undemocratic and arrogant. Cleaners are people, too, you know. And that is what inspection should be all about.

Inspectors feel that they probably need to spend less time (only just though) looking at the building and grounds. Of course, if an inspector is talking to a resident in the resident's room then they can inspect this personal part of the building while involving a resident. This is a good use of time and is, as we'll see in the case study descriptions below, a favoured tactic of inspectors. Nonetheless, I believe too much time is spent zooming around a home, in some half-crazed surveyor-like manner, hunting out with a feverish zeal the sub-standard sins of the building: searching out the shoddy, the shabby, and the stale; ferreting out the filthy, the faulty and the flawed; burrowing through to the botched, the bungled and the badly done. Once again, I think this is symptomatic of inspectors feeling the need to do their job 'properly'. They all know that no home can be perfect, so they have to find something wrong. Finding something 'wrong' = doing a good job. A worrying formula.

Interestingly, this was not lost on providers. Indeed, a few that were interviewed confessed even to deliberately leaving something for the inspector to find. 'It's lovely to see their faces when they find it,' said one provider mischievously. It's a shame that inspectors can feel obliged to feel this way, but it must surely be considered a failing. The need for at least one recommendation to make it to the report is a need inspection could do without: it can do little but polish up inspection's negative image. Surely, also, minor repairs can be sorted out with a quick word from the inspector and even quicker deed from the provider. I know of cases where this has happened but the 'fault', although sorted during the inspection, is still reported (and no doubt checked upon again at the next inspection). The inspector could report that minor repairs were discussed with the manager who carried out some immediately and promised to make good the others within the week. The unnecessary detail is gone, the inspector has let the world (their boss) know that they've been doing their job 'properly' but has also acknowledged the responsiveness of the home – which is a fair indicator of the quality of the home's practice. Everyone's a winner. And baby, ain't that the truth?

what providers say

So, how do providers believe the inspection pie is carved up? The findings were very similar to those of inspectors.

during an *announced* inspection, roughly what percentage *is* spent doing the following tasks? Also, what percentage do you think *should* be spent?		
task	% of time **actually** spent	% of time you feel **should** be spent
talking to residents	7	17
talking to relatives (including advocates and other representatives)	3	8
interviewing the manager (or person in charge on day of inspection) or owner	35	29
interviewing care staff	7	11
interviewing support staff	1	3
inspecting records and administration	29	17
inspecting the premises	13	11
inspecting catering arrangements	5	4

Far too much time, say providers, is spent on interviewing the owner or manager and looking at paperwork, and far too less spent with residents. Interestingly, whereas inspectors say they spend about 14% of time talking to residents, providers put it at half of this at just 7%. However, whereas inspectors suggest that this should be as much as 21% of the inspection, providers suggest a more cautious target of 17%.

According to providers anything up to 75% of an inspection is spent with the owner or manager. To be fair to inspectors, though, there are providers who slavishly follow inspectors around by choice ('trying to lose my marker' is how one inspector described such a situation). One provider explained that 'unless a resident wishes otherwise the owner and their representative should accompany the inspectors and hear what is said and see what is inspected.

Inspectors forget that they do not own the managers and the premises. They are paid for by a service industry and that industry has a right to service not policing.'

Inspectors felt that they gave the manager, owner and paperwork about 58% of their time at an inspection, whereas providers put it at 64%. Inspectors thought it should be 43% and providers 46%. Providers are still keen, it seems, to be involved (and perhaps positively influence) an inspection.

Providers also felt that too much time (but as with inspectors, not *that* much time) was spent inspecting the building. They say about 13% of time (which is about an hour of our average hypothetical inspection) is taken and perhaps it should be 11%. Harold Wilson famously said that a week is a long time in politics. I will suggest, less famously, that an hour is a lifetime in inspection. I know that buildings are indicative of the care and that safety is important, but these buildings have already been registered. Only changes to it need be hunted out. The rest can be seen as the inspector goes about their real job – finding out from the people who live, work and visit the place. Unless there are concerns, even the largest home should take an inspector minutes. If there's something good to see or if there's a problem one of the people that the inspector talks to will surely alert the inspector to it. Inspections shouldn't hinge on hinges, they should open doors for people.

One provider obviously believes that an inspector knows best (three cheers resound around all unit offices): when asked how should an inspector divide their time up during an inspection bravely replied 'whatever the inspector feels they should do'. Now there's an inspector's ideal provider.

some things to think about...

...when inspecting

- think about how much time should be allocated to an inspection and think about how best that time should be spent. Consider what should be at least a minimum amount of time for each type of inspection. Consult on this and publish it.

- you can't hope to cover everything, so be honest and say what you covered and how: think about a disclaimer for your reports.

- consider the importance of people and allocate time in relation to the importance you place upon them.

- involve **all** people who live, work and visit a home in an inspection.

- minimise the time spent looking at paperwork and the building.

- remember that people may well be nervous about having things to say, so be approachable, friendly and smile (a lot).

- do your best to fit around with the home's daily routines: remember it's the residents who are the most important people in a home, and not the inspector (sorry).

- remember you don't **have** to find things wrong – if a home's doing really well, say so, and don't resort to petty recommendations.

- oh, and **never** call basic information 'principally static information'.

case studies

case study, number 2

an inspector calls in...
Newcastle-upon-Tyne

It is the (commendable) policy of Newcastle's Joint Inspection Unit 'that all inspections will be undertaken by two inspectors', one of whom will be the lead inspector. Inevitably this means a pre-inspection chat between the inspectors about tactics and priorities. This well managed unit, while understanding their regulatory role, take a great pride in the developmental side of their work. As one inspector said: 'I think we're there as enablers rather than inspectors: it's unfortunate that we're called that. We're promoting good practice. Give praise. Don't make out that we know everything.'

The inspection for one inspector starts as their car is parked: 'how does the building look? The gardens? The initial impression.' The bell is rung followed by 'greetings, introductions and a few minutes of pleasantries.' One inspector felt that their 'demeanour at the front door in the first 60 seconds is crucial: smiling, shake hands if appropriate.' It is important to 'get the inspection off to a good start.' The philosophy seems to be "keep it pleasant, keep it courteous but keep it professional." The lead inspector would introduce the second inspector and the lay assessor.
Time is spent early on explaining the process, negotiating a routine or timetable and so on. It is felt important to help relax the manager as they are 'just as twitched as everyone else' and recognise the fact that 'anxiety levels shoot up during inspection.' In an attempt to create a relaxed atmosphere one inspector said that they will 'have tea and biscuits with the manager, an informal 20 minutes, talk about developments in the home.' Another said that they would 'use 10/15 minutes to build up a relationship: general banter, take care of practical issues – "you can still go the toilet" – and start with some open-ended questions: "Do you want to kick-off? Anything you want to tell me?"' Another said that 'we take great pains to explain the process – take the drama out of it.'

Inspectors have 'a pro-forma to work through' and divide the work between the two of them: the lead inspector is office-based and works on the paperwork ('a sense of need to get the bureaucracy out of the way'), the second inspector will 'tour the building doing a building check.' However, during an unannounced inspection, inspectors will go 'straight around and do the building – look at care practice.'

Back at the announced inspection, the lead inspector will 'work through statutory records: identify people with high dependency needs/recent admissions (4/6 care files) – a fairly holistic approach – trawl of residents through their care plans into quality of life issues: social assessment, life, career, likes and dislikes.' The lay assessor is usually despatched to the communal areas with staff to meet the residents. Talking to residents is largely delegated to lay assessors on announced visits. However, one inspector was clear that this was very much their job as well: 'the most important aspect is talking to residents: watch them talking – is their eye contact on me or the manager? If the manager stands by me they won't talk.' Another inspector felt it important to have 'a break at lunch time – even if only for 15 minutes.'

The inspection is concluded with a feedback session, so that there are 'no surprises in the report.'

some thoughts on the

good stuff

importance placed on getting inspection off to a good start

open, friendly approach to inspection

importance of involving residents

tracking residents' care back to their files

reassuring and explaining

strong team spirit and management

feedback at the end of inspection

and just

some thoughts

can more time be allocated to residents?

think about the importance attached to the order in which things are inspected and what time should be allocated

> why is lead inspector office-based and the second inspector out-and-about – should this not be the other way around?
>
> why do people look at care practice while inspecting the building and not look at the building while inspecting care practice?
>
> think of ways to include residents in the feedback session at the end of the inspection

how do inspectors engage residents?

General chit-chat: what's for dinner today? Who are the staff on duty – do they know the names of staff?

Staff are kind but rushed. You get stock answers. So you observe their non verbal communication, body language, tone of voice, whether they are over hearty in that Butlin's-type of talking down. Staff getting their own way in a nice, caring kind of way. Hold hand while talking to them.

Get down to residents' eye level. Use a footstool. Small talk.

With the tv blaring, it's no good trying to speak to them.

Introduce myself, say why I'm there – see how everybody is, what's it like living here...

Naturally for someone who believes the residents are central to the inspection process, I find it truly remarkable that a provider can say that 'on my last inspection no residents were spoken to.' That's an inspector who drops a little short of the definition given by another inspector: 'got to be a people person but intuitive, vigilant and tenacious.' Well the resident-avoiding inspector probably is intuitive, vigilant and tenacious when it comes to lunch breaks, time-off-in-lieu and car mileage claims.

As we've already seen, inspectors may spend little or no time with residents during an announced inspection, leaving that part of the process, in the main, to lay assessors. These inspectors then tend to use the unannounced inspection to concentrate time with residents. As one inspector said: 'Unannounced inspection allows time for me to sit down and take quality time: what I call the 'quality' inspection.' And another: 'Announced inspection is when I am least available to residents.' But this is the inspection that residents, hopefully, are aware that an inspector is coming. They might have taken days to prepare themselves for what they might like to say and the inspector spends more time looking for evidence of a Regulation 14 visit than with them.

Admittedly I have not seen that many posters advertising an inspection, but many of them say something to the effect of 'we would like to hear what you have to say'. I have yet to come across one that says: 'The inspector regrets to announce that despite the fact that they are spending the best part of a day inspecting this home, they will not be able to meet with any residents because they have got more important things to do. We do not mean to be unco-operative, but your co-operation towards our unco-operativeness will be appreciated. PS We will get around for a chat at the unannounced inspection but we can't tell you when that will be.'

I will tell staff if I feel I had a good day and inspection.

Use leading questions. Ask if they have got a good view in their room and what's it like. They will then ask if you would like to look at it.

Horses for courses. Helpful to see people in their own rooms. This gives the chance for icebreakers – talk about the room, talk about the photographs.

Sitting, come down to their level, that's if they're willing to talk to you. Do it there in the lounge or go somewhere private...'get out of the way of the television'...'bugger off!'

However, even if inspectors are able to talk to residents, it must be recognised that residents aren't always willing, ready or able to take part in an inspection. As one inspector said: 'Some don't want to chat.' A number of units make it clear in their guidance that residents need only take part in the inspection if they wish to, and, indeed, use letters and posters to inform residents about that. Certainly, in everyday situations, inspectors have no right of access to a resident without their permission. However, sometimes residents choose not to take part or feel they shouldn't because the process hasn't been explained to them clearly enough or pressure, no matter how unintentional or indirect has been brought to bear.

This is why it is crucial that inspectors look to build a relationship of trust with residents. And you get that by getting to know the names of residents and their families; being friendly, polite and happy; being genuinely interested in what they have to say; letting them know what will happen (or what has happened) as a result of them telling you things; using words that are easily understood by them; chatting to them at first about what's important to them and not firing off a rat-a-tat set of questions like 'So how long have you been here? Have you a tenancy agreement and are you able to challenge its conditions? Do you feel empowered to make representations or raise issues that affect the quality of your placement?'

all dressed up...

Also, what an inspector wears can have an affect on how you are treated by residents. In Barking & Dagenham, I wanted inspectors to be dressed in a casual but smart way. Indeed, I did. I broke a 406 year tradition at the civic centre when I stopped wearing a tie to work. There were mutterings in the corridors of power but nobody said anything. I wanted the way inspectors looked to reflect our unit's preferred informal approach. Suits were banned as they smacked of officialdom. While inspecting children's homes, I would wear a sweatshirt, jeans and trainers. However, I remember being told off during an inspection of one home for older people for being scruffy (I wasn't wearing a tie). It was then that I realised that inspectors had to dress accordingly for each client group. A jacket and tie was okay for a home for older people, because it was *expected*, people in authority should look like they are. However, looking like someone in authority can be very counter-productive when visiting children's homes, homes for people with mental health needs, or homes for people with drug or alcohol dependence. Again it proved to me that standardisation should exist separately for client groups and not across the board. We deal with people not computer parts.

good to talk?

Even when inspectors do meet with residents, this does not guarantee that the inspector will get the information they are after. One inspector said that 'you can get people's life story: interesting as it may be, it's not great information.' But it does help with building a relationship. Some residents might not realise that they have anything to say to an inspector. Some think that they are being inspected and act accordingly with guarded, one-word answers. Still, your number might be up and some might chat away nineteen to the dozen when one-to-one, and within two shakes they'll have gone the whole nine yards and left you at sixes and sevens. Still, that figures.

It can be easy to talk to residents and it can be difficult, very difficult. More so, for those residents who have difficulties in communicating verbally, but we will look at how inspectors involve those residents in the next section. Here we're going to look at how inspectors ordinarily engage residents.

In homes for older people, for example, you might come across a group of residents sitting in the lounge, an unwatched tv squealing with a tellytubbies' group hug fills one corner, in the distance a vacuum cleaner drones breathlessly on, and the residents, backs safely guarded by the wall, stare at nothing to see. And then the inspector arrives. The situation is as unreal as real can be. One inspector pointed out the everyday anxiety of such situations: 'I still take a deep breath – how am I going to be received? Look around and see what eye contact I get – see if I get a smile returned.' A bright and breezy, cheery and chirpy *hello* from the inspector followed by a careful look for eye contact seems to be the best ploy at this point. As one inspector carefully observed:

> *It's very hard to talk to someone when everyone else is listening. Wait for significant eye contact. Don't say straightaway 'if you had a concern what would you do?' Prefer: 'how are you today?'; 'how long have you been here?'; 'is there anything you want to change?'; 'how do staff treat you?'. Talk about their room and they might offer to show you which means you can also get to speak with them more privately. Don't put issues in their mind, I want them to tell me, not to have me prompt it out of them.*

Similarly another inspector explained:

> *No note books, leave them to one side. Take your jacket off...if no seats get down on hands and knees – seek their permission. Use icebreakers: weather, what they had for lunch, general conversation before what do you think of the place, the facilities, the staff. Use touch, reach out holding hands, see how they react. Keep reassuring them who you are and why you are there. Tell people a little about yourself – are you married, do you have kids, etc.*

Both these inspectors display great understanding, sympathy and skill. The eye contact and sitting down next to residents is, quite rightly, the preferred technique. As another inspector importantly noted: 'If I stand up then I'm talking down to people.' One inspector said they 'Say *hello* to everyone – when you get eye contact, make your way to that person. Sit next to them if a vacant chair. Observe. Watch how often staff walk past or pop in to say *hello*.' Another inspector makes an important point when saying they 'sit down with residents, come down to their eye level.' They follow this up by having 'a cup of tea, try to jolly them up a bit – "anyone sitting out in the garden?"' However, they are aware enough to add that the residents 'get tired so I don't outstay my welcome.'

Whether inspectors should eat with residents is, for me at least, surprisingly contentious. Many inspectors appear not to. As one said: 'I observe resident/staff interaction – don't eat with them.' And another: 'I haven't ate with residents. I'd like to but haven't.' Outstaying a welcome or feeling intrusive are, perhaps, understandable reasons given why some inspectors do not eat with residents. Inspectors having their own break cuts less cloth for me.

As an inspector you never really stop working – sometimes the work is very pleasurable, thank you very much, sometimes it is quite relaxed, other times it can be stressful. You might want a few minutes to think through some things you've heard or seen, then take a 10 minute walk in the gardens or to the shops – to see what's available nearby. If you were on your way home from work and you saw a resident being dragged back into a home, you wouldn't think 'oh well, it's 5.15, I'll pop around next Thursday after our team meeting to see if everything's all right.' You would go and investigate immediately. The point is, in one sense, you're always on duty. I don't expect inspectors to take breaks during an inspection unless really necessary. You can recharge your batteries while looking at files (inspectors spend enough time in offices) – it's probably boredom that pushes them to having breaks. But surely not at significant times of the day in the life of a home? And meals are the home's main (sometimes only) social events of the day. It really is too good an opportunity to miss. It's a great chance to observe staff under pressure (as they usually are in bigger homes) and a good chance just to chat. Some inspectors feel that such chats are contrived. But they are as contrived as you make them.

I even feel pangs of disappointment if staff do not eat with residents, eat the same food, or sit at the same tables. So this is multiplied many times for inspectors. I recall one inspector that I visited a home with (which was transferring to my borough through local boundary changes) thinking it odd that I should want to spend lunch time with residents rather than in the office with the manager who, it has to be said, had laid on quite a spread for us. The inspector being a vegan also said, with a delightful non-intrusive motivation, that they preferred to bring their own food because homes wouldn't have the strict foods required. I, in my best what's-that-got-to-do-with-the-price-of-the-fatty-substance-obtained-from-cream-by-churning, carnivorous way, suggested that might tell you a lot about a home. So, if a vegan turns up at the home on an emergency placement: what are they to eat? How would the home cope? What would they do? Do they know what a vegan would eat? And so on.

So, to teach me a lesson, I'm sure, I was strategically placed at a table with two very confused residents: one who was convinced that their son (she didn't have one) was coming today to take her home; and the other (who was 91) who wondered aloud and frequently what time mummy would be coming to dinner today. She didn't turn up.

Eating with residents can be informative, interesting and fun. As one inspector said: 'If residents are happy, we eat a meal with them [paying for it]. Two separate places are set for inspectors. We participate in the social event. It's a way of life now: homes expect it.' The paying for the meal is a small but important detail. If a home, as many do, refuses payment then offer a donation to the residents' fund or something similar. It is a very important detail in impressing an inspector's integrity.

Involving residents in the inspection process – even if that process isn't particularly people-focused – has got to be basic, fundamental practice. One provider was particularly upset about a shift in their inspection unit's policy: 'I was happy with inspection until recently when the emphasis changed from residents as priority to property and buildings.' Enough said.

residents with limited communication or understanding

Talking with them, sitting with them, observing their lifestyle and contact with staff.

In a variety of ways though we are often reliant on the staff in the home to facilitate this.

Observation.

I try and allow more time to listen, make sure I express myself simply, try and involve friends, relatives and carers. Observe.

Interviews and postal questionnaires from inspectors gave a pleasingly strong picture of their respect for the dignity of residents who have limited communication skills or understanding. As we have seen it can be difficult to stimulate residents who are lucid and able to talk. Naturally it follows that those residents who are not, require even greater patience and skill. Most recognised that these residents should be treated equally as other more able residents. As one inspector said: 'all residents are entitled to the respect of the inspector.' It means giving more time, taking longer to pick up signals through expressions and body language, observing how staff talk and walk with them. As another inspector said: 'I would talk to confused residents in the same way as other residents. You can still establish something. If not verbally, you can see their facial expressions.'

It is intriguing that there appears to be very little work – in ways of practical training – being done by inspection units or, being on offer for communicating with residents. Again, perhaps this reflects something about the role of people in the inspection process. Having said that, I was genuinely moved by the attitude of inspectors interviewed as part of the case studies. Their statements that they would simply 'spend time with these residents' and not by-pass them as unproductive were uplifting. As one inspector put it:

> *First thing you need is patience. Listen carefully. Ask staff to help me: get tips from them, that sort of thing. With confused older people, timing is important. You need patience. Reading between the lines, body language, anxiety levels can be picked up.*

*By getting them to show you their own room and possessions and by really **listening** and taking time with them.*

Try to make sure that staff are available to interpret or reassure client.

Learning disabilities – I may ask if a resident would like to show me around the home, or if anyone would like to show me their room. This gives opportunities to talk about various topics. If someone is confused sometimes I may sit and hold their hand, listen – talk a little, look at expressions – body language.

I always sit with residents and where they have difficulty in communicating, I take the opportunity of observing staff practice. It is also important to involve relatives or advocates, and people are informed in advance about the inspection, so that appropriate others can be there to give feedback about the quality of support.

With the EMI [elderly mentally ill] it is difficult to get answers – observing how staff interact, their availability, what residents look like, how agitated behaviour is dealt with.

Find out from staff learning disabled residents' basic signals for yes and no. I talk to confused residents as with any other. Use observation skills: do staff spend time with them.

Sign language, gestures, Makaton.

I remember two quality assurance staff carrying out an audit on transport provided for day care services who decided that they wouldn't issue questionnaires, talk or interview clients because of the nature of their disabilities. It was a remarkable arrogance compounded by saying that they took this decision in the best interests of the clients. I think not. They took it in their own best interests because consulting with clients seemed just a little bit too much like hard work. So, I drafted in independent inspectors and local advocacy groups to carry out the consultation with the people who actually used the transport. They just might have something to say about it: it might just take a bit of time to say it, that's all.

Indeed, at one of the day centres an inspector spent hours with one client because of the difficulty in communicating. The client had a lot to say about transport and was particularly pleased that somebody had taken the time not only to ask but also, crucially, to listen.

Time is the key. However, this, in itself, is a cause for concern as inspectors – particularly those with heavy workloads (which as suggested earlier to be over 25 homes) – are forced to shorten inspection time. And given that, on average, inspectors spend a small percentage of that time with residents anyway, there must surely be a fear that inspectors will look to improve the efficiency of an inspection and choose not to spend time with residents with communication difficulties.

One inspector said: 'Give **more** time. Make sure there is somewhere quiet to talk with not too many distractions. Occasionally ask for staff help. Seek views of relatives/friends who have regular inputs and contact.' However, another admitted that 'we are not particularly pro-active in this difficult area,' but recognised, nonetheless, basic observation is important: 'Direct observation of staff interaction with residents can be very telling. Many confused people can offer some comment about their care.'

case studies

case study, number 3

an inspector calls in...
Northamptonshire

Inspectors recognise that the 'whole job can be intimidating: need to cause as little disruption as you can: we're not here to make it a bad experience.' An inspection begins with a knock at the door and showing the ID card. Then 'introduce myself – talk to who's in charge – tell them why I'm there – try to get home relaxed.' The lay assessor is also introduced and is used as an ice-breaker, as the inspector asks the 'manager to give lay assessor a run down of home.' The inspector then takes the lay assessor away to meet the residents.

The inspector keeps the atmosphere relaxed by having a 'general chat with the manager – how things have been since last inspection – anybody poorly – explain what I would like to do.' This involves time with the manager and checking records.

Then follows a 'tour of total premises with manager – sometimes use care staff: this gives a chance to talk to them also.' Inspectors are aware that they are 'there for care staff as well. It's about building up relationships with staff – attend staff meetings and so on. This helps minimise impact of the visit on staff.' The manager or staff member introduces the inspector to the residents: 'learning disability and physical disability and children are more likely to come to you – older people are less ready to talk.'

The inspector will 'book lunch. For learning disability and mental health homes, I'd go at tea time.' The inspector will open a fire door and ring a call bell to test staff response times.

Unannounced inspections are 'more a look at quality of care from a resident's perspective: observe practice and chat with residents; look at care plans and residents' records; and any outstanding issues that need to be covered.' The inspector will 'wander around and introduce self to residents: general chit chat with them – how do they find things? Did they know they were coming? If it's my first visit I would look at the terms and conditions of residency.' All inspections end with verbal feedback.

some thoughts on the
good stuff

importance placed on getting inspection off to a good start and causing as little disruption as possible

reassuring and explaining

eating with residents (with their permission)

involving all staff in inspection

good management

feedback at the end of inspection

and just
some thoughts

can more time be allocated to residents?

think about involving residents more – in showing inspector around, in feedback

think about the importance attached to the order in which things are inspected and what time should be allocated

human nature? inspectors and instincts

Gut reaction counts every time: walk through a door and it's there.

It is natural, isn't it? You walk into a hotel, pub, club or whatever, and your brain is bombarded with messages. You like the look of this place; you aren't sure about the feel of that place. We've all done it, haven't we? And more often than not, I would guess that that first impression, that first *instinct* has not been too far wide of the mark.

Should inspectors use their instinct? Yes, most assuredly. In any case it would be hard not to. Some things we do are simply instinctive. Should inspectors rely on instinct? Absolutely not. But, as one inspector put it, 'instinct is only a starting point.'

It can be most infuriating: you know it's not right but you're damned if you can find it by the end of the visit. But when you uncover what you've been unsure about then there's something satisfying about that.

An inspector walking into a home will get a feeling immediately. Whether the home is warm or cold (physically and otherwise), quiet or noisy, buzzing or deserted, bright or dark, will all be registering strong messages in that little regulatory brain. An inspector will have a feel for the home – whether good, bad or indifferent – but will have to hunt and capture the evidence to prove (or disprove) that feeling.

In my days as your local inspector on the beat, my starting point always was *would I be happy for my mum to be here?* If I thought I could leave my mum there, I would then need to work out why I would. If I thought no way, similarly, I would need to work out why. At least one inspector agrees with me: 'Although I am cautious about instincts as you never see the full picture, the best benchmark for me would be would I be happy for my mother to be in this home? But not part of the inspection process – I would need evidence.' Indeed, it's important to be sure that any judgement made was safe and not one presided over by prejudices, preferences, preciousness and various other social conditionings beginning with 'pre'. One inspector asked if they used their instinct, replied: 'Can't say you don't. I don't make decisions on them (but consumers would). I need to look further to find evidence.'

Go with atmosphere, with hunch.

You get that gut feeling – you're receiving messages but not sure what they are. You need to work out why you think that way.

I use my instinct a lot. Within a few minutes you have a definite 'feel' for a home.

Our perception of the word *instinctive* is a fairly positive one, we think it has a good sound to it. As we do, generally, with other words that describe it: *automatic, subconscious, spontaneous* and even *gut reaction*. All of these are warm, positive feel-good words (sort of): they are *natural*. However, a *knee-jerk* response, which is also instinctive and natural, carries with it a whole different baggage. It's unthinking and is not a good thing at all. So, although natural, wholesome and pure (a sort of Cliff Richard of the senses), instinct should not be allowed out on its own. As one inspector put it:

As soon as I walk in the door, my feelings start. That's human nature.

> *There is a thing about instinct – the feel of the place, the atmosphere. If staff are hostile or guarded, straightaway you start to think 'why?' But I don't rely on instinct. Inspectors have been fooled – not hard to do, I know – you think a place is good then a complaint comes in and shows you that things are horrendous.*

Gardens tell you a lot. Is the home fresh and warm? Decor, cheeriness of staff – are they pleasant when they open the door – helpful?

We have already touched on the subject of easy-to-judge stuff (three bedrooms, one toilet) and hard-to-judge stuff (quality of life experienced by different people): the quantitative versus the qualitative. This essence of this debate, which has raged on and ravaged the regulatory landscape for, oh I don't know, must be hours now, is whether inspection is seen as art or science. Is it hard, concrete, factual, and objective or is it less tenuous than that? Is an inspector an artist drawing on skill, aptitude and expertise to paint the bigger picture? Or a scientist testing a home against systematic observation and classification, leaving judgements on the back (Bunsen) burner? Certainly department of health thinking – if *The Briefcase* is a testament – would favour the latter approach. An inspector's task is to uncover evidence that sits down with the facts and stands up in court.

I use my instinct a lot, that nurse's intuition. I've walked in and thought 'whoops, don't like this!' But have to find evidence.

You do. Mix together the instant reaction and the vibe, but can't leave without finding out why.

Yeah, all the time, all the time. You've got to follow your instincts, and you've got to be able to back that up with evidence. Having worked in the sector, you know what's stage managed.

As ever, with all these things inspection is neither art nor science and yet is both these things. There can be little doubt that there is a place for the qualitative and quantitative: a scientific approach to gathering facts *about* things and people (in that order), coupled with the inspector's art of collecting information *from* people and things (in that order). As one inspector said: 'Instinct plays a part. You get that feeling that something's not right. Inspection is a science in many ways but there's also a touch of art about it.'

But perhaps the last word on instinct should go to this very obviously scientific inspector: 'Touch wood, my instincts have not been wrong yet.'

whose side are inspectors on?

We asked inspectors whose side they thought they were on. Did they see themselves as champions of residents' rights? Here are some of their comments.

Not on any particular person's side. You could say that I'm on the same side with the manager and proprietor – we want to get the best for residents. We mustn't lose sight of the fact that on the whole providers are doing a good job.

Trying to feel what it's like being a resident, but I can't.

We're all there for the clients.

Change should not be sought for the sake of it. There has to be a need for change. That means you have to understand that need and be able to explain why it needs to change.

I do think we are advocates in one way of residents' perspectives.

Wear all hats. Fight for residents (if indeed they need fighting for). Staff need protecting as well. I'm there as an adviser to the manager, and an enforcer.

That's the motivation – championing of rights.

A good home is one that raises the expectations of residents.

Advocate, whistle-blower, residents' champion: that's my job.

On the side of residents – a sort of advocate, really.

We're there for the residents but we achieve through staff.

Residents don't see me as championing their rights, we're not that upfront. It's important to let people know we have a role and our relationship has to be with the owner/manager.

case studies

case study, number 4

an inspector calls in…
South Tyneside

On homes with 20 or more beds, South Tyneside use two
inspectors: the lead inspector being office-based with the co-
inspector out and about (although these roles are reversed
annually). Homes with less than 20 beds are inspected by one
inspector. Each inspection kicks off with the 'common
courtesies: hello and introductions and a little chat.' On
announced inspections, inspectors phone the home to tell them
they are on their way.

Great emphasis is placed at the start of an inspection on
'working towards making it as relaxed as possible: you know,
"we're here now and let's try and make the best of it" sort of
thing.' It's policy 'to get as many staff together at start and
explain the process. Remind them of the offer of a chance to
speak to us. Get staff to introduce themselves – this helps
breaks the ice.' The inspectors feel they are 'upfront about what
we tell them: "we're not here to criticise you – here to inspect,
here to observe."' Inspectors 'find out who's poorly' and if there
are 'any areas we shouldn't go in.' Inspectors also 'make sure
that the lay assessor is comfortable' making sure that they
'understand their role and remit.'

Inspectors spend less time with records than perhaps most
units. As one inspector explained: 'every home has a policy and
procedure file kept at the unit. A month before the inspection
homes have to say that they have reviewed their policies and
procedures and send a note to say "no change". This saves
about an hour at the inspection.'

After interviewing the manager and checking records,
inspectors have a look around the premises. This time is used to
observe practice and routines – 'how escorted to toilet – is it like
a conveyor belt?' The unit feel that they have less emphasis on
buildings and more on people. Indeed, on accompanying an
inspector on an inspection, a resident, on being asked whether
she knew the name of her inspector, said 'Oh yes, I know [gave
name], she's like one of the family.' Inspectors join residents for
meals in homes (if a larger home only one of the two inspectors
– usually the lead inspector – will take a meal, along with the lay
assessor). This is unit policy because 'people tell things better'
during social events.

Time is also spent 'talking to all staff on duty'. One of the aims of the unit is to 'identify and disseminate good practice.' As one inspector said: 'talk to staff: any good practice, routine, activity that you do – that I won't see – tell me about it. Ask about innovative or new practice that you're proud of.' This is a very positive approach to inspection. As another inspector said: 'we compliment and commend.'

The inspection ends with a feedback session between the inspector and the manager or owner or both. Inspectors explain what will find its way into the report. The feedback is also written down and either copied (if the home has a photocopier) or sent out by the next day: 'we do this because sometimes homes are so tense that they don't really hear what you have to say.' However, one inspector would tell the manager or owner the requirements and recommendations that would be in the report but does not say what commendations will appear: 'I tell them it's good but don't actually say it will be commended in the report.' This is because there have been times when what seemed on the surface good practice but after later reflection or further evidence uncovered was not so.

some thoughts on the

good stuff

importance placed on getting inspection off to a
good start – involving as many staff as possible,
good ice-breaking techniques

positive, friendly approach to inspection

importance of emphasising residents over buildings

tracking residents' care back to their files

reassuring and explaining

good team spirit and stable management despite
temporary management arrangements

good efforts made to reduce amount of time on paperwork

keen to find out good, new and innovative practice – particularly
those things that might not be seen at the inspection

written and verbal feedback at the end of inspection

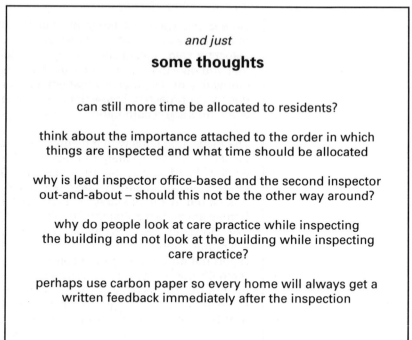

and just

some thoughts

can still more time be allocated to residents?

think about the importance attached to the order in which things are inspected and what time should be allocated

why is lead inspector office-based and the second inspector out-and-about – should this not be the other way around?

why do people look at care practice while inspecting the building and not look at the building while inspecting care practice?

perhaps use carbon paper so every home will always get a written feedback immediately after the inspection

lay assessors

the Barking & Dagenham experience

There probably hasn't been a more controversial, worrying or threatening development in the inspection process than the introduction of lay assessors – members of the public who accompany inspectors on certain required inspections. An all-embracing, singing and dancing, unresearched, without proof or foundation assumption: but, I suggest, a pretty damn safe one. Five years or so on, and lay assessors are still causing grief, anguish and suffering: can't recruit 'em? won't recruit 'em! They are eyed nervously (are they after our jobs?) or suspiciously (what is their motivation?) or unreservedly contemptuously (I'm not having him!).

I never knew what the fuss was all about. I only wish that I had thought of it – and sooner. I believe in local democracy and accountability (fear not, I shall spare you the tormented socialist tract) and believe in the concept of public service: you know, *serving* the *public*. I also believe in the need for inspection units to be open, honest and transparent in their work. So, involving volunteer members of the public is an excellent way of reflecting positively all those beliefs. Add to that that they also help to raise the profile of the unit (underestimate the power of word-of-mouth at your peril) and the mix is delicious.

No sooner had the enthusiasm gripped me for this that I suddenly stuck with pangs of doubt. What was I thinking? This idea will go down a storm in the leafy suburbs of retired, moneyed-folk, Women's Institute do-gooders and their ilk, causing the three-tiered cake stand to positively quiver with anticipation, but in depressed, deprived Dagenham? It would hardly muster the interest to slip off the top of a Tupperware bowl. One inspector has had a similar experience in their area: 'I think our lay assessors are "too professional". We don't necessarily target the right people. I haven't met an ordinary working class person or housewife – they all come from professional backgrounds.'

Nonetheless, convinced the idea was sound (but equally convinced that nobody would reply, and just as equally convinced that I was about to invest a lot of time and money that may be as beneficial as imposing a hose pipe ban in the desert) I wrote and published a glossy magazine: Do You Have A Fresh Point of View? The title was naff, but not as naff as the colours used: blue and orange. I liked the magazine idea. I also liked the fact that it was an odd shape – longer and thinner than A4. It stood out. Best of all, it worked. Within three months we had sent out 26 application packs, received 18 back, appointed 16 and began to turn down further applications – figuring 16 was way enough. We then decided to use members of the public on all inspections (we only inspected full day care nurseries of children's day care services at that time) and so looked to recruit parents to help inspect nurseries. The last campaign I embarked on again used a magazine format – two pages from which are shown on pages 136–137. This was left in places such as supermarkets, job centres and chemists as well as the more usual places: libraries, GP surgeries, hospitals and so on.

By the time I left Barking & Dagenham, we had 32 lay inspectors on the books. Admittedly 12 of those were approaching the end of their shelf lives (as they called it), but pretty damn pleasing, nonetheless. We consulted them on what to be called, with lay inspector being preferred to lay assessor: so that was that.

The use of lay inspectors was, I believe, hugely successful. There were some run-ins at times but, for me, that was what it was all about. There was no point in having 32 clones. But, above all, I like to think that our lay inspectors knew that they were valued, that we believed in what they did and in what we did, and as a consequence, so did they and so they stayed. People will quickly pick up whether you're sincere or just going through the motions – and will respond accordingly. We used lay inspectors on all inspections – children's day care included – from the start. We thought if the idea is good, we should apply it to all services.

I encouraged lay inspectors to write their own reports rather than have it form part – or as the jargon seems to have it – subsumed into the paid inspector's report. I wanted them to have a voice and have their say. No more powerful was this than following an inspection of a private nursery. The inspection was over two days with a different

the things they say

*Some quotes from
our lay inspectors*

"I remember feeling nervous and unqualified"

**One of our lay inspectors,
Cheryl Cullen, talks about what
it's like being a lay inspector.**

*"The residents
seemed very
happy and at
home during my
visit"*

I was browsing through a local paper, when the recruitment advertisement for lay inspectors caught my eye. It's not often you see a job advertised that isn't looking for previous experience or relevant qualifications.

The inspection unit were looking for people who had no professional experience of residential care. I had no experience at all. All I knew about residential care homes was that the elderly lived in homes for the elderly, children live in children's homes and so on.

*"I was impressed
with the new
system of drug and
medicine care,
which left little room
for error"*

However, at the time I was a counsellor in training and thought that the skills I had acquired during my training could be applied to the role of lay inspector. At the same time I thought that this was an ideal opportunity to practice and enhance the same skills.

*"If this is care in
the community
then let's have
some more".*

I also believed my own childhood experiences provided me with a certain amount of insight regarding children that have themselves experienced the world as less than ideal. In addition, I had also grown up with children and adults with learning disabilities. So although not in a residential setting, I had in fact interacted with "very special people" all my life.

I gathered up this bundle of experience and skills and offered them to Graham at the inspection unit. I'm happy to say they were welcomed and appreciated.

*"The accommodation
was extremely clean
and of a very high
standard"*

The first home I inspected was a home for adolescent boys. I remember feeling nervous and unqualified. However, the independent inspector was there to meet me, brief me, and then throw me in at the deep end. In hindsight, I now know that it was my lack of experience and insight into residential care that produced the curiosity needed to conduct the inspection.

---

lay inspector (both parents) on each day. The findings were appalling. The paid inspector's report was clinical and matter-of-fact: standard after standard was not met. But when read in tandem with the sheer horror and disbelief of the parents' reports, the effect was devastating. The inspector had written from the head, the parents from the heart. The nursery closed down.

As the time for the first wave of lay inspectors came to the end of their three years, it seemed to me absurd to say goodbye, thanks a lot see you around, to these people who had picked up such experience and understanding. They still wanted to offer their time for free. I had to

I had absolutely no idea regarding the rules and regulation and the practices of the home, how certain issues were dealt with or how privacy, dignity and empowerment were implemented. However by talking to residents and staff, (sensitively) participating in meals, and activities through general observations, I was able to pull together an idea of what the home was about.

At the end of the day I could write a report of my findings and then follow this with my "independent point of view".

"There's one question I always ask - would I be happy with the service provided if it were for a member of my family"

It would be misleading to say that this is how I conduct every inspection, every inspection is different because every home is different. The service is provided around the particular needs of the residents. For example, in one home I might spend an hour playing nintendo with a child in care, while at a day centre I might participate in a sensory room session.

However, there is one question that I ask myself during all inspections. Would I be happy with the service being provided if it were for a member of my own family? This question can be referenced back to many aspects of a residential care home or day centre. For example, is the food

appetizing, balanced and varied? Is the interaction between staff appropriate positive and sensitive? If I was concerned over a particular issue I might bring it to the attention of the manager for discussion. Or if it was of a very serious nature I would bring it to the attention of the independent inspector to be dealt with appropriately.

However, the answers I end with, whether negative or positive will go into the report supported by my independent view. One of the most important objectives during my inspection is to conduct the inspection in a courteous and unobtrusive manner. The bottom line is that this is someone's home and should be treated with respect.

The process of inspecting a home and then writing up a report is hard work, and in all probability adds to the already busy life that my colleagues and I lead. However if you're interested in people, a people person, then the position provides an opportunity to meet many people from many walks of life, in varied working and living environments.

Apart from the role of lay inspector allowing you to work in an area that is fast changing, interesting, and in general an enjoyable learning experience, it gives you the opportunity to act in some way, in the world you live in, and especially for others who might have fewer opportunities than yourself.

the things they say

Some quotes from our lay inspectors

"My only recommendation is that they acquire a new three piece suite as the existing unit is in excess of twenty years old"

"I have to say that I am not a Health & Safety expert but I will highlight the problems which as a mother I find unacceptable in an environment accommodating young children"

"All the residents I spoke with appeared to be satisfied with the home"

"All residents are encouraged to place keepsakes and personal items of property in their rooms"

find something else for them to do. One idea was for them to become 'friends' of a couple of homes and visit them (with residents and the homes' permission) regularly. They could then be interviewed as part of the inspection process, being able to give a broader picture of life in a home. Another (more obvious one) was to kick them upstairs into one or both inspection advisory panels (or *groups* as we voted to call them). They had open invites to these groups anyway but were there as interested people rather than voting members (not that I ever recall a vote being formally taken).

However, the idea I began to pursue was setting up a lay inspectors' management group. This would mean that ex-lay inspectors would 'manage' and recruit and select lay inspectors in partnership with the inspection unit. I would, in effect, contract members of the public to attract and provide other members of the public to act as lay assessors. It seemed ideal. It improved their independence, it would take a lot of the everyday work with lay inspectors away from me, and would again give people a sense of worth and value. Unfortunately, my departure also meant that the idea, although well grounded and approved (bravely, I thought) by social services committee, did not reach fruition.

However, so well-established was the idea and use of lay inspectors that at the last inspection conference, providers voted as a suggestion for improving the inspection process to allow lay inspectors to visit homes at different times to the paid inspectors. Which was nice.

lay assessors – the principle and experience

Gets out of hand, they start coming into the home pretending to be the inspector.

Valuable part of the process. They are, in my experience, highly skilled, caring and motivated people.

Mixed – some who are superb: they look, talk and learn: spend lots of time with residents. Some don't seem to know their role. It's a good concept – I'm pleased to have them.

Very valuable. Come up with some constructive points.

Clearly inspectors were concerned at the introduction of lay assessors. The government's statement that they would bring a fresh, common sense point of view upset many inspectors who took it as a slur that their views were foolish, unrealistic and stale. Nonetheless, despite these first doubts and concerns, it seems inspectors are happier and feel that the work of lay assessors is, in general, positive. As one inspector said: 'First I felt fear and trepidation about how it would work – a lot of anxiety. But certainly here it has been excellent – a positive part of the process.' Another inspector admitted: 'I was against it in principle because I doubted their motivation. I felt that they were there to inspect us. It was a slur on my professionalism and I was suspicious of that bleeding Tory government. I did fear a take-over from retired colonels. But have changed my views. It has worked well in practice, generally very positive. I have managed to tolerate and even enjoy the vast array of reports we get.' Providers, too, said one inspector were less than sure about the involvement of members of the public: 'In the beginning providers had a lot of suspicion: staff were spooked by them.'

Another inspector 'had doubts about lay assessors in the beginning. No-one likes change: there was a shadow of a threat, but it's been a positive experience. In the announced inspection they can do the bits I can't do.' Indeed, this seems to be the case for a number of units. Lay assessors have the time to speak to residents that inspectors believe they themselves haven't. As one inspector explained: 'It's a very good principle involving ordinary people – very valuable, yes. In fact without them our inspection protocol for announced inspections would be ridiculous, but with a lay assessor available they are able to talk to residents.' I do worry about this use of lay assessors. It's not that I doubt their ability but I do think lay assessors talking to residents should supplement the inspector's time with residents and not replace it.

Having said that, chatting with residents is what lay assessors do best. As one inspector said:

Inspectors were uncomfortable with them but I am comfortable. I think they are a good idea and they should be used more. Some, though, are an embarrassment. Lay assessors are a bone of contention here – they always come up at meetings – inspectors saying they don't want them anymore.

I agree with the principle: it has been a positive thing. But there's still this 'official thing' – she's the inspector: have you come to inspect me? Have we passed?

Very positive. More than we could have thought. There have been a few problems but has worked very well.

They ask naïve questions that are good.

Campaign once a year: write up in local newspaper (which also goes into the free papers); application pack; two 'preparation afternoons' (existing lay assessors come along for the second afternoon to tell them what it's like); handout booklet; if no response send questionnaire out asking why not.

One had an insensitive approach: in a young person's room he began to open drawers and wardrobes.

Every inspection report sent out to the public includes a leaflet asking if they would want to become a lay assessor.

Residents in old people's homes enjoy having lay assessor to talk to. In a mental health home, for example, they often only deal with people in authority: manager, doctor, nurses, officials, inspectors. Lay assessors do not represent any professional agency. Residents didn't want to talk about waiting for flats, employment or medication, they wanted to talk about themselves.

However, inevitably some lay assessors have attitudes that upset inspectors and providers. As one inspector said: 'Some could do without the attitude (school governess type of thing) but they do well.' And a provider thought their lay assessors were 'more suited to a Buckingham Palace tea party.' But the same could surely be said for some inspectors and providers.

We asked inspectors whether they agreed with the principle of using lay assessors. Of the 30 that replied:

do inspectors agree with the principle of lay assessors?		
comment	number	percentage
yes, fully	7	23%
yes, mostly	15	50%
yes, partly	6	20%
no, not at all	2	7%

While not a resounding thumbs-up for lay assessors, nearly three-quarters of inspectors were at least mostly happy or fully happy with the principle of lay assessors.

We asked providers whether they agreed with the principle of using lay assessors. Of the 114 that replied:

do providers agree with the principle of lay assessors?		
comment	number	percentage
yes, fully	35	30.7%
yes, mostly	36	31.6%
yes, partly	29	25.4%
no, not at all	14	12.3%

Perhaps not surprisingly, there is less comfort among providers over the principle of lay assessors. Just over 62% of providers say that they are either mostly or fully happy with the principle. However, over a third of providers are only partly happy or not at all happy over the use of lay assessors.

We asked inspectors to describe their experience of lay assessors. Of the 26 replies (actually only 24 replied but one inspector gave three answers):

how do inspectors describe their experience, in general, of lay assessors?		
comment	number	percentage
excellent	4	15%
good	13	50%
okay	8	31%
poor	1	4%

Just under two-thirds of inspectors describe their experience of lay assessors as good or excellent. Interestingly, one inspector who said that they disagreed with the principle of lay assessors reported that their experience had been good.

One inspector had clearly worked with three lay assessors and graded each differently. The lay assessor that was graded 'poor' was done so because of their inability to get reports in on time. Something that a bona fide, fully paid up professional inspector would never do. No, sir.

We asked providers to describe their experience of lay assessors. Of the 86 that replied:

how do providers describe their experience, in general, of lay assessors?		
comment	number	percentage
excellent	14	16.3%
good	28	32.6%
okay	29	33.7%
poor	15	17.4%

Just under half of providers have found their experience of lay assessors to be good or excellent. Just over a third rated their experience as okay, but nearly a fifth rated their experience to be poor. However, the interesting point for me, is that five years on, 29 providers (a staggering quarter of those surveyed) had never experienced lay assessors.

other thoughts on lay assessors

As with most things to do with inspection, the way that lay assessors are used seems to differ from unit to unit. Do lay assessors write their own reports or are their views part of the overall report? Do they get to see previous reports or the pre-inspection questionnaire? How much 'training' (this taboo word is always in quotes but, in essence, it is what most lay assessors get), guidance, information, preparation do they get?

In Barking & Dagenham, our lay inspectors got together (they had support group meetings every three months) and wrote a guidance booklet recognising that they were all different in their needs and wants: some were very confident and did things their own way, others almost wanted to be led by the hand. A good idea I came across in **Newcastle** was the introduction of a buddy system – where an experienced lay assessor accompanies a new lay assessor to help them settle and to judge their effectiveness. As an inspector said: 'We have less of chance to talk to residents so lay assessors do it, but it's not always the same, they miss things. It's a good principle having lay people representing the general public. But there's a lack of 'training'. Communication skills: in one hour and watching a video – you can't do it. In practice, I'm happier this time because we've used a buddy system to help new lay assessors and see how they do; you know, find out if there's any hidden agenda, their motivation.'

good practice	*'buddy' system for lay assessors*
	Newcastle use experienced lay assessors to 'buddy' up with new lay assessors to help them through the inspections and also to help assess their potential effectiveness.

The reports written by lay assessors can be a source of excellence, embarrassment and amusement. The freedom that lay assessors have to say things staggers across a tightrope line between an inspector wishing they could say those things, and falling despairingly into a cringe-pit. As one inspector concisely put it: 'lay assessors can say stuff we can't.' Another inspector said: 'I have limited experience of lay assessors, but based on that I have been very impressed. Their reports are better than ours. The language is down-to-earth, gutsy.' This straightforward my-point-of-view approach can be refreshingly powerful but can, of course, be counter-productive.

I recall a lay assessor writing something to the effect of 'THIS HOME STINKS OF URINE. THIS IS TOTALLY UNACCEPTABLE.' The lay assessor was right: the home did smell and the smell was unacceptable. But it was the manner of saying it that wouldn't work (not least the use of capital letters): it would simply get the backs of the home up and we'd have two entrenched, heels-dug-in no-way-out deadlock. And while I would never change a lay assessor's report I would talk to them about the impact of such style and language. If they wanted to keep it, then fine. But at what cost? They would have to go to that home again and that would cause an uncomfortable if not downright hostile atmosphere. My approach always was to ask the writers of contentious comments – how would they feel if someone said that about them? And about the manner in how it was said? What did they want to achieve? Did they want the smell (or whatever) to be put right? If so, how about a more restraint, explanatory approach? Yes, say the home smells and that it really shouldn't, but don't get high and mighty about it.

I had sight of another inspection unit's lay assessor report, the tone and manner of which should form part of a manual of 'How Not To…'. The report opened with the bizarre line (although in quotes I am quoting from memory): 'What have [name of home] and Minneapolis International Airport got in common? Smoking is only permitted on the tarmac.' And the rest of the report lived up to this start memorably. The chef was described as being 'unable to draw much water'. An inspector said that lay assessors 'can write inappropriate things. One once wrote: "Don't queue here, folks."' Another inspector noted that 'We keep plugging away at them to write more about what the residents say. You know, *you* might *think* that but what do the residents say…?' Perhaps sound advice for inspectors and assessors the world over.

There is an excellent role that lay assessors can also play which would supplement and improve an inspection unit's process: they could be recruited to reflect a local population that is perhaps missing in the inspection team. There would be little sense in sending a white, middle-class male inspector to a children's home for young black women. Similarly if there are homes run for Asian, Jewish, Catholic or other ethnic groups or religions, and those backgrounds or cultures are not present in the inspection team – then try to recruit people from those communities as lay assessors.

The same goes for people with disabilities and other users of service. As one inspector, who described their experience of lay assessors as 'extremely good', said: 'I think disabled facilities are okay but disabled lay assessors show they are not.'

The involvement of the public can be invaluable but for it to have any hope of being successful, the inspection unit has got to be committed to it. And if they are, then they will surely start to look at new, different and innovative uses of the volunteer support they get.

case studies

case study, number 5

an inspector calls in...
Suffolk

Suffolk have detailed protocols for all inspection and other regulatory activity. This inspection design, despite its bureaucratic nature, rooted as it seems to be in the unit's wish to achieve the international standard for quality assurance – ISO 9002, makes clear the expectations of inspectors and improves the unit's consistency. Although I have doubts about the true credibility of ISO 9002, Suffolk intend to bolster that with Investors in People and the Citizen's Charter – so all aspects of their work achieves external verification. Suffolk designs its inspection process in a rounded, comprehensive and coherent way. An example of this is their impressive closure process.

During the announced inspection, after 'knocking and waiting' inspectors move into the manager's office (except perhaps one inspector whose preferred style of inspection is 'walk and talk – I don't like offices'). Inspectors like to strike a balance between the formality and informality of the day: 'easy-going but not pally. Don't frighten them to death – no point in dictating.' Efforts are made to help relax the atmosphere from the start. One inspector said that they would 'ask the manager to say what improvements have been made – start off as positive as possible – an informal catch-up with things' and confirmed that they do 'spend a lot of time with manager.' A good tactic to break the ice was described by one inspector: 'if there's a lay assessor, invite the manager to tell them about the home.'

Then during inspecting records, inspectors identify 'most in need residents and follow through the care of those individuals.' This is an excellent inspection tactic. The lay assessors are used mainly to talk to residents. If there is a lay assessors present, they will be encouraged to eat with residents; the unit always paying for their meal.

The afternoon is usually set aside for a 'tour of the building' usually with the manager or a care assistant. When asked why they weren't shown around by a resident, one inspector said: 'go off with resident? If they would let me; would like to, but it doesn't happen.' Another inspector explained their afternoon-with-residents technique: 'knock on doors and have chats individually – say hello to everybody and shake hands – I want residents to see me – "that's the guy" I want them to think.' However, the inspector admitted that he would 'meet people with the manager.' Inspectors agreed that it is best not to make notes while talking to residents as this would be too distracting or disconcerting for residents. It is better to make notes afterwards. Inspectors also carry business cards to leave with residents and relatives – and this excellent practice has been very successful. It has also helped raise the unit's profile – as has their sponsorship of bookmarks which are given away free in the county's libraries – an excellent innovation.

Announced inspections have, in keeping with the inspection design, a very formal approach. Unannounced inspections are seen as more informal where inspectors only spend 'one hour with the manager' and can 'sit with residents.' All inspections end with verbal feedback.

some thoughts on the
good stuff

detailed and rounded inspection process

importance placed on getting inspection off to a good and positive start – good ice-breaking techniques

tracking residents' care back to their files

reassuring and explaining

good team spirit and strong management

detailed inspection guidelines ensuring consistency

good thought gone into balancing the formal and informal approaches to inspection

verbal feedback at the end of inspection

and just

some thoughts

can more time be allocated to residents?

think about the importance attached to the order in which
things are inspected and what time should be allocated

why do people look at care practice while inspecting
the building and not look at the building while inspecting
care practice?

if the formal/informal split for inspections is the
preferred option, perhaps the announced should be the
informal inspection

verbal feedback

It seems that giving verbal feedback to the provider is a well
established part of the inspection process. Inspections are nerve-
wracking times for providers and the occasional update to let them
know how it's all going can be very helpful – even if there are some
critical things being said. People just prefer to know how or where
they stand.

We asked providers were they given feedback and when, and 115
providers responded as follows.

when are you given feedback during an inspection?		
feedback	number	percentage
throughout the inspection	22	19.1%
at the end of the inspection	34	29.6%
throughout the inspection and at the end	57	49.6%
no feedback given	2	1.7%

Interestingly, nearly a third of providers say that they don't receive any feedback until the end of the inspection. I am not sure why this should be the case. I am sure that it isn't the inspector playing power or mind games, but it could easily be perceived that way. I am also sure that if inspectors saw some poor or unacceptable practices that they wouldn't wait until the end of the inspection to bring the issue up, but would look to deal with it there and then. Similarly if something really good is seen, why not compliment it at the time you see it? Not knowing how the inspection is going is clearly a frustration for providers. One provider suggested 'feedback throughout the inspection' as a way to improve the inspection process. Another said that 'it would be helpful to receive more feedback during an inspection rather than have to wait for the end.'

We asked inspectors when they provided verbal feedback during an inspection, and 29 replied as follows.

when do you give feedback during an inspection?		
feedback	number	percentage
throughout the inspection	0	0%
at the end of the inspection	6	21%
throughout the inspection and at the end	23	79%
no feedback given	0	0%

All inspectors said that their verbal feedback was given to either the owner, manager or senior staff on duty. Four inspectors said that they would routinely feedback to the staff group and one said that they would do so occasionally. Only two inspectors said that they would feedback to the client group as a matter of routine (although this was more likely to happen at a children's home), two would on occasion and one would 'as appropriate'. Again this re-enforces the reality that inspection is seen and delivered as primarily a tool for management.

how happy are providers with inspection and inspectors?

The overwhelming message from providers is that they are, in general, happy with inspection and the way that inspectors conduct themselves. There are undoubted gripes ('no matter how positive some aspects of the visit are, the focus is inevitably negative'), real concerns ('inspectors do go into residents' rooms when the residents are not in them, an invasion of their privacy'), and many suggestions to make things better ('stop wasting time by going over the same things'). But, on the whole, our research shows a general contentment out there. Many providers view inspection as positive even if in an indirect way: 'Makes you do those things that you keep putting off.' One provider saw inspection as a 'way of keeping us on our toes and making sure we keep up to standard.' Any inspector worth their salt will want not only to see providers on their toes, but to see those toes twinkle.

Despite bad experience with one of their inspectors (described as 'extremely bad – enough to consider legal action') one provider was still very happy with the process and the way inspectors conduct themselves.

We asked providers if they were happy with the way their homes are inspected at the moment. Of the 115 who replied:

comment	number	percentage
yes, very happy	50	43.5%
yes, it seems all right	53	46.1%
not really	10	8.7%
no, not at all	2	1.7%

We also asked providers if they were happy with the way
inspectors conducted themselves during inspections. Of the 115
who replied:

comment	number	percentage
yes, very happy	**64**	**55.7%**
yes, it seems all right	**38**	**33%**
not really	**12**	**10.4%**
no, not at all	**1**	**0.9%**

We should not under estimate the potential effects of an inspection
visit. One provider spoke about the 'negative experience' of their
last inspection. The previous two were described as 'very
productive'. However, during their last inspection, the provider was
critical of the inspector's inter-personal skills and that only 'negative
things [were] identified', with the inspector offering 'no positive
feedback'. And this in spite of good standards. The inspection was
described as 'very demoralising'. It is fair to say that the experience
of inspection as far as a provider is concerned hinges very firmly on
the approach and character of the inspector. As the same provider
noted: 'perceptions are coloured by the personality of the
inspector'. Indeed, in response to the question *Are you happy with
the way inspectors conduct themselves during an inspection?* one
provider certainly spoke for many when he replied: 'Depends on the
inspector'.

It is surely possible that even the most difficult or critical inspection
can be viewed as positive, fair and even inspiring if the manner of
the inspector is open, clear, reasonable and polite. Most inspectors
interviewed agreed that even in a home that was clearly failing, they
would look for some positive things to say. Feedback (preferably
during the inspection but certainly at the end) should include things
that the inspector thinks are working well, show potential, or are
appreciated. Not only is it reasonable to expect this to happen but it
also gives heart and shows that the home can do well. This
approach must be better than hitting a provider over the head
repeatedly with a catalogue of inadequacies. Only when it becomes
transparent that a provider is still failing despite all support, advice
and reasonableness should the head bashing commence
(figuratively speaking, of course).

The cold, clinical listing of failures and required action in a required time has its place in the inspection process: it's the last chance saloon tactic. It should not be an everyday part of inspection (which is more of a friendly, welcoming snug, I suppose). Effective inspection is like effective management: it's all about getting things done with people. And things are more likely to get done in an atmosphere of respect, understanding and warmth.

after an inspection

chapter 6 – after an inspection

...we now work to a huge list of standards. The resulting reports are just a long list of ticks with a few comments added here and there. Reports give no flavour of individual projects and we feel that everything has to be "standardised" not unique or individual...I would like to get away from the "tick box" where you're either right or wrong back to a more collaborative, open way of working where differences of opinion are acknowledged and respected

manager of a voluntary home

at a glance

this section looks at:

the inspection report

providers comments

monitoring inspectors and inspection

introduction

As if the experience of being inspected isn't enough to deal with, the poor provider now has to suffer the suspense of waiting to see what the report actually says. Sure, they have had feedback but it probably never sets them up for seeing the whole thing written down in black and white (or black and blue – an interestingly combative combination – if you're in **Cambridgeshire**). And as if having to go through the intensity of carrying out an inspection, the poor inspector has now got to go back, sort out all their notes, make some sense of it all and put it all down in black and white, Cambridgeshire excepted. This chapter deals in the main with the beast known as the inspection report.

the inspection report

Alfred Hitchcock (well I did mention the word *suspense* above, so I feel it's highly appropriate, and anyway, whose book is this?) is attributed to have said 'Drama is life with the dull bits left out.' It seems Hitch's cast-offs (the dull bits) have found a retirement home: inspection reports. I have read thousands of them over the years from many different inspection units and I don't think I'm giving away any trade secrets when I say how dull they are. Some, I am sure, have been written by King Dull of the Dull People of Dull-land. If we ever develop a dull-seeking missile…oh, well, I think the point's made.

There are reasons why inspection reports are dull. First up, perhaps inspectors are simply not so good at writing, and their discomfort shows. Also, there's the 'everything could end up in court' lobby who cause inspectors to write in third-rate police-speak (an achievement, let me tell you). The (very real) fear of litigation from providers, or more likely the fear of it by legal sections and the council's insurers, has also encouraged a devotion to blandness, where judgement has no place. This is a serious problem for some units and seriously limits their effectiveness. But, in my view, the main reasons that inspection reports roam free in the bland-lands are because, in general, they are target-less and lack clarity in purpose which causes them to be pompously-written, jargon-filled and poorly designed.

Many inspectors say report writing is the part of the job they dislike the most. For them it's monotonous, tedious and, well, dull. Now if the author of something is uninspired by it, pity the poor reader. As Dr Johnson said: 'What is written without effort is, in general, read without pleasure.' And you can't knock the boy Johnson on this. But report writing is the backbone of inspection, it's what keeps everything else up. Someone who dislikes report writing should not be an inspector. It's like a mechanic who can't stand engines. It's what you do. Inspection is not just part of the care industry, it's part of the communications business. And while an inspector might moan that this is their 25th inspection report that they've written this year, they should remember that it is the home's first – and it is (probably) eagerly awaited. If inspectors put themselves in the shoes of the prospective readers of the report, this might spark some inspiration, care and effort on their part.

However, I am sure that inspectors' dislike for report writing is founded on the expectations placed upon them (real or perceived) rather than any inability to write well. Writing is a skill that doesn't get the attention it deserves or needs. Most inspection units will have an inspector, usually a senior (in years, at least), who everyone else believes to be the font of knowledge about English. They are grammar-driven in a grammar-less society and, as such, are revered because everyone else lacks, in varying degrees, confidence in writing. Trouble is, their style is usually turgid and formal. Add to that the fear that your written word will embarrass you or expose insufficient knowledge, eminence or (oh lordy) professionalism, and the mix makes for pomposity beyond belief. But it really doesn't have to be like that.

When you think about it, if you are trying to communicate clearly to the world what it's like living in a home, that's a skill and a challenge. To find the words that adequately describe or analyse your collected evidence and observations, should be a treat not a chore. And so it would be if inspection reports actually set out to do that. But, sadly, the evidence suggests otherwise.

the three questions

Before a word of an inspection report is written, the inspector needs to be clear on the following three questions:
- what is the purpose of an inspection report? (why are you writing it?)
- what do you want to happen as a result of your inspection report? (what outcomes do you want to achieve?)
- who is your target audience? (who are you writing it for?)

the purpose

There are five reasons why we write. These are:
- to inform
- to find out
- to record
- to persuade
- to enforce

The main purpose of an inspection report is to **record** the findings of the inspection. However, an inspection report might also seek to **inform** various people about the home and to **persuade** providers to adopt any good practice recommendations made in the report.

Therefore the style that an inspector uses will have to take these things into account. A bright, clear, positive and friendly style will help an inspector inform and persuade. Ultimately, of course, an inspection report may be used as part of the local authority's decision to **enforce** a course of action upon a home. In this case, which is a very small minority, a more formal tone would be necessary.

the outcome

This will vary, but we can assume that inspectors will want homes to take credit for any good practice, to take action on any requirements and to respond positively to any recommendations that are made. Either way, the standards in a home will be maintained or, better still, improved. Again the manner and tone of the report are crucial to achieving this. Don't assume that a recommendation made will be understood and carried out. Explain why it will help.

target audience

During interviews, inspectors told us who they write inspection reports for:

I use nursing specialist language as the report is a tool for home.

For employers.

Main aim is for owner/manager but bear in mind you want relatives and residents to read them.

Who are inspection reports written for? This possibly causes inspectors most confusion. There's no easy answer they say. They write reports for a wide variety of people. Their managers, the providers, residents, relatives, staff, legal sections, councillors, commissioners, purchasers, and, of course, the general public. As one inspector said: 'If it is the only record of the inspection it needs to meet many requirements; I feel this is difficult to achieve and to ensure that the report remains comprehensive and understandable to staff, carers, residents and the general public.' Quite simply, if an inspector is unsure who they are writing for, the report will suffer. The choice of words will depend on the knowledge of the reader. And be clear about this, it is the writer's job to make things easy for the reader. So if the target audience is the manager, then using a term like *keyworker* is fine. If the target audience is the public, *keyworker* is not so fine and will need to be explained either when it is used or in a glossary.

It is impossible (perhaps) to write a report to please everyone. It's not impossible to write a report that everyone will understand, but this, say inspectors, would be patronising to providers and other professionals. This snobbish dismissal of what is (ironically patronising in itself) known as the lowest common denominator takes my breath away: like having people understand what you have to say is somehow demeaning. More like a fear of being found out, I'd say, if I was being deliberately cynical. I have heard of a social worker resigning as an inspector because they felt being 'told to use small words' in their reports (the unit was committed to plain English) was an insult to their professionalism. And of another, who on being told that 'social role valorisation' was not a phrase the public would understand, barked 'well, perhaps it's time that the public did some work on this.' The arrogance is deafening.

In my old unit, where two successive temporary heads of unit tried (valiantly) to keep the plain English flag flying, one independent inspector was disheartened at having his reports sent back for rewriting. 'Don't worry,' consoled the head of unit, 'it's not just you, I have to do it to everybody else as well.' To which, the inspector replied 'Well, if you have to do it to everybody else, haven't you thought that you're wrong and we're right?' Inspectors moan about poor uptake of reports by the public. But is it so surprising given that they probably don't understand a word? Sometimes, I feel that plain English is a flag flying over the social services equivalent of Rorke's Drift – with wave after wave of jargon warriors needing to be repelled. It would certainly be easier to surrender: is this bravery in the face of adversity or sheer stupidity? While I work that one out, pass another sandbag. Hurrah!

Try to write it bearing in mind someone will read it in a library as a choice of home.

So, who **are** inspection reports aimed at, and who **should** they be aimed at? We asked inspectors and providers to grade each of the following target audiences in order of importance for inspection reports. The most important target audience was to be scored with a 1, the next most important a 2 and so on until the least important target audience which would score a 9. This means the **lower** the average score the **more important** the target audience is. This is how inspectors and providers think it is at present:

First it's my formal record of the inspection; secondly, the owner; then residents, staff, relatives and public.

inspection reports target audience	how it is: inspectors	how it is: providers
	average score	average score
head of inspection unit	3.7	1.9
legal section	5.9	4.7
director of social services	5.2	2.9
general public	3	4.7
carers, relatives or representatives	3	4.3
elected members	6.3	5.7
providers	1.6	3.9
staff	3.5	5.9
users of service	3.3	5.6

For general public, but I've never met anyone who's ever read one.

The disparity between how inspectors and providers see inspection reports is telling. Inspectors aim reports at providers in the main, whereas providers think they write for the head of inspection unit. Providers also think that users of the service, staff and the general public are way down the list of importance for inspectors. However, inspectors believe they target the public, carers and users only after providers in importance.

This is how inspectors and providers think it *should* be:

inspection reports target audience	how it should be: inspectors	how it should be: providers
	average score	average score
head of inspection unit	4.6	4.1
legal section	6	6
director of social services	5.1	4.8
general public	2.5	4.6
carers, relatives or representatives	2	2.5
elected members	5.5	7.2
providers	2.3	2.8
staff	3.2	4.2
users of service	1.7	2.4

Primarily for the manager/proprietor – I'm being realistic because that's where 90% of changes are going to occur.

If I was prospective resident, would I understand it?

Inspectors and providers (just) agree that users should be the most important target for inspection reports, with carers second most important and providers third. The only real disparity of ranking between inspectors and providers is that given to the general public. Inspectors ranked the public as the fourth *most* important target, while providers thought the public third *least* important.

I write for the public.

In Barking & Dagenham, following consultation, our reports were aimed at the public (which, of course, meant residents as well). We made our reports look more attractive (colour covers, simple, clean design) and wrote them in plain English (or the best approximation I could coax out of our inspectors). However, our reports were long, and no matter how nice and easy to read they may have been, 30 plus pages simply wasn't user-friendly. Thus entered the summary report. We asked the public what they wanted to know. They said 'what do you think of the home and what services has it got?' So that's what they got. Simple, really.

The essential thing for me here, which had been crawling around my mind, but which now burst through in all its messy glory, was that the public **wants** us to make judgements about a home. So we told them what we thought (and why), what services the home offered and where to get a copy of the full report if they wanted one. And in four pages (A3 folded) of large type. These were sent out free to all

For anybody who wants to read them.

residents in a home, with a few extra for the home to distribute. We also put reports on tape and sent those out. The project I was working on when I left was reports in pictures for people with learning disabilities, which would not be posted out, but delivered by the inspector, who would talk to them about the report, what it meant and what should happen as a result.

It is, of course, excellent that providers and inspectors think that users of services should be the main target of reports. But the reality remains that nothing, if very little, is done to make reports meaningful for residents. But the starting point has got to be plain English.

plain English

As I have said, writing is a skill. Writing in plain English, however, is a specialised skill. It doesn't mean using just words of one syllable. This book is written in plain English – or at least the bits I've got control over. For example, this paragraph scores 89 on the Flesch scale. This is a scale that rates the readability of written English. The scale runs from 0–100, with 0 being unreadable and 100 being very simple. Plain English is said to be about 60 on this scale.

Plain English means being clear, using everyday words, avoiding jargon and being concise (we'll look at examples of these from inspection reports below). It also means using short sentences (look to average about between 15–18 words a sentence) and being human.

being clear

When recording or writing to inform (as with inspection reports) it is important to be clear. The reader must be able to understand exactly what you mean and at the first time of asking. It's not the reader's job to make sense of what you say. The reader is hungry for information, and by serving it to them on a plate you can still present it well and make it tasty.

However, sometimes what we say can be misinterpreted. This is often because of a badly constructed sentence or the use of words that mean different things to different people. Inspectors responsible for the following examples all presumably thought what they had to say was clear enough, but the construction of the sentence allows a different, sometimes funny, interpretation.

> *Young people do not express dissatisfaction with their rooms but the fact remains that they appear small and uninviting.*
> That's children for you.

> *Staff confirmed that residents go to bed when they choose.*
> Bossy staff.

Wardrobes within bedrooms are not always fixed to walls to prevent crushing accidents and this is recommended.
Required, surely?

The inspection concentrated on an attempt to become acquainted with a sample of residents.
My advice is never get acquainted with residents' samples.

First Floor – Dining Room – The floor covering is severely scarred.
It's emotionally wrecked – it's not got over the death of the rug. They were very close, you know.

Residents are offered a choice of menu for every meal and individual requests can be catered for.
Not really funny, but I just like the use of 'catered for' when talking about food.

Temazepam is stored in the CD cupboard.
Yup, in between Technotronic and The Temptations you will find the Best of Temazepam.

It's a matter of concern that no cook's post has been provided on the establishment. There is no gardener or handyman post either.
Well, maybe it's just that no-one's written to them…

…and a Salvation army choir will be introduced to the home. This will be monitored at the next inspection.
Hallelujah.

In addition, staff escort residents to hospital appointments and have access to a key worker.
I'm sure the staff need one.

The next couple of examples are using words that have different meanings.

The Inspector felt that staff were concerned over health care matters and that the needs of the residents are being addressed.
The use of 'concerned' could mean the staff were **worried** about health care matters or were **interested** in them.

Some of these job vacancies are outstanding.
I'll say. £22k a year for a care assistant? That's brilliant, is that.

And some where the wrong word is used or a typing error gives us a wrong word.

> *All of the residents who were able to express an opinion made positive comments to the inspector about the variable choice and portion size of the food.*

'Variable' means not steady or regular. Perhaps 'variety of' just sounded too simple.

> *The proprietor is required to keep a register or all patients in the home and this is satisfactory.*

The *or* should be *of*. I think, anyway.

> *The acting manager is keen to adapt and implement the recommendations.*

Can't just accept them, then? *Adapt* should read *adopt*.

jargon

I'll just give two examples, here. This from a health trust that wanted to find out what their patients thought of their service. But to say that would be too simple...or, should that be too difficult?

> *This framework for establishing patient/client interface needs to be constructive enabling us to hear views that might not otherwise be heard so influencing the strategic direction and day to day experience of clients/patients.*

And this from an inspection report:

> *It is acknowledged that the balance between supporting independence and respecting residents' rights, challenging accepted norms and identifying areas of need, so as to facilitate responsible and planned risk taking, is complex.*

You're not kidding.

everyday words

The way that people try to show how eminent they are is through using pompous, big or posh words, instead of dead simple, ordinary, everyday ones. This simply says 'look at me, I am so much better than you.' In writing inspection reports the task is not to impress but to inform. An example of this pomposity is the use of the word *methodology* when explaining how an inspection was carried out. It is a word hijacked from the world of academia (the only true language of self-inflated importance) and sounds so much more professional than *method*. Other examples from inspection reports with simpler alternatives are listed below.

> *The inspection concentrated on a systematic scrutiny of the premises...*

The inspection looked closely at the quality of the buildings and grounds.

The menu showed a provision of quiche and the manager thought that possibly no-one had chosen that provision.
Quiche was on the menu but the manager didn't think anyone had chosen it. (Who would? Real inspectors don't eat quiche. Quiche is for wimps).

The staff in the home have put in a lot of work since the last inspection to make the transition (move) *to the existing premises* (new home) *as smooth as possible.*

...the Home's Aims and Objectives need to be fully reviewed to ensure that the text and terminology (wording) *is appropriate for residential care.*

Beverages (drinks) *are provided at set times and upon request.*

Residents preferences are documented.
Residents' likes and dislikes are written down.

The complaints procedure was requested at the Home by a relative and this had not yet been actioned.
A relative who asked for a copy of the complaints procedure has yet to receive one.

The hot water delivered to the baths was in excess of the required temperatures.
The water in the baths was too hot.

being concise

It's a good guide to use only the number of words you need to make a sentence work. This doesn't always mean using the fewest possible, however, as sometimes a few extra words help to make things clearer. For example *Inspection Methodology* is one word less than *method of inspection*. But I know which is the clearer. It's a question of swings, roundabouts and bouncy castles. I think. Here are some examples of over-wordy sentences from inspection reports, with suggested alternatives.

In the circumstances please ensure evidence is in the future retained for this purpose.
Please keep records from now on.

The garden area to the front of the property was found to be in a unkempt, overgrown state.
The front garden was overgrown.

The home have a complaints procedure and this is displayed in the home.
The home's complaints procedure is displayed (say where).

*A small enclosed garden at the rear of the home provides an
area where service users can sit out. The need for a door mat
by the back door was identified.*

Service users can sit in the small, enclosed back garden. A
foot mat is needed by the back door.

*The Inspecting Officers were able to examine the Patients
Register and were satisfied with the content and accuracy of
the information recorded.*

The patients register was accurate and well kept.

*I spoke to several residents who expressed satisfaction with
the care they were receiving and praised the quality of the
food served within the home.*

Several residents said they were satisfied with their care and
praised the quality of food.

Enough said.
Sorted.

being effective

Inspection report writing always seems to liven up if judgements are
made: where inspectors get to say what they think based on the
evidence. However, this appears to account for very little of
inspection reporting which remains largely repetitive, bland and, at
times, irritating. Take this example:

SECTION 8 – MANGEMENT OF HOME

f) Does the home have a Residents Committee or series of
residents meetings?

Yes

When I read this all it sparked in me was a hundred unanswered
questions, such as… How often do residents meet? How many times
before? Who attends? How effective is it – are decisions followed up,
if so, by who and how? Are minutes taken – who by, were they seen,
are they easy to understand, who gets copies, where are they kept,
are they agreed by meeting? Are meetings run by residents,
advocates or staff? How are they advertised? And so on.

Also, when inspectors need to make points, they should do so
tellingly. Perhaps more so than this:

SUMMARY OF MAIN FINDINGS OF THIS INSPECTION

The summary of findings of this annual inspection are that actions are required by the registered person in all areas of the homes functioning (there are 44 in all) and it is matter of great concern that some fourteen of these actions were raised at the annual inspection of July 1997 and despite improvement once again required to be improved again.

The use of plainer English and clearer thinking could turn that example into this:

Summary

There are a number of concerns about this home. The inspector has listed **44** areas of action that the home **must** act on and a further **7** recommendations that will also help improve the quality of care provided. It is also very concerning that **14** areas of action are being repeated from last year.

The home has made some headway in the past year but as this report clearly spells out, there is still a long way to go.

But perhaps the last word on effective reporting should go to this example:

In what ways are residents encouraged to pursue individual hobbies and interests?

Encourage residents to continue with any hobbies and interests.

writing a report

As already said, inspectors can find report writing uninspiring and time-consuming. But how much time is actually consumed?

We asked inspectors how long it takes them, typically, to write an **announced** inspection report? The 30 that replied did so as follows (one inspector gave two answers):

how long does it take to write an announced inspection report?					
length of time	1–2 hours	3–4 hours	5–6 hours	7–8 hours	9–10 hours
number	**4**	**13**	**8**	**4**	**2**
percentage	12.9%	41.9%	25.8%	12.9%	6.5%

It's safe to assume that most reports take up to a day to write. Naturally, some reports will take longer if there are concerns or there just happens to be a lot to report. No doubt there will be some envious eyes clocking the four inspectors who can knock out their reports in two hours or less.

We also asked inspectors how long it takes them, typically, to write an **unannounced** inspection report? The 30 that replied did so as follows (one inspector gave two answers):

how long does it take to write an unannounced inspection report?					
length of time	up to 1 hour	1–2 hour	3–4 hours	5–6 hours	7–8 hours
number	**3**	**13**	**9**	**4**	**2**
percentage	9.7%	41.9%	29%	12.9%	6.5%

As to be expected, the shorter visit means a shorter report taking four hours or less to write. Most inspectors reported that it takes only a couple of hours or less to write. However, for a couple of inspectors a full day is needed to complete their unannounced reports.

when are reports delivered?

Given that either announced or unannounced inspection reports are generally written within a day, how soon after an inspection are these delivered to the home? This is a big issue for many providers. And some of the waits reported cannot be seen as anything other than unacceptable. One provider said the inspection process could be improved if inspectors would only 'send reports more promptly.' Another provider agreed: 'Quicker after inspection reports'.

We asked inspectors how long after an inspection, typically, is an inspection report delivered to a home? The 30 that replied did so as follows:

how long does it take you after an inspection, typically, to deliver a report?					
length of time	1–2 weeks	3–4 weeks	5–6 weeks	7–8 weeks	9–10 weeks
number	8	18	2	1	1
percentage	26.7%	60%	6.7%	3.3%	3.3%

Nearly 90% of inspectors said they get their reports to the home within four weeks. Reports should be delivered as soon after the inspection as possible, and a month should be ample time, ordinarily, to achieve this.

We also asked providers how long after an inspection, typically, is an inspection report delivered to them? The 117 that replied did so as follows:

how long does it take after an inspection, typically, to receive a report?					
length of time	1–2 weeks	3–4 weeks	5–6 weeks	7–8 weeks	9–12 weekss
number	14	52	23	10	12
percentage	12%	44%	20%	8%	10%

Six providers (5%) also gave the following answers: 16 weeks; when ready; longer!; variable; three months +. The difference between inspectors and providers is marked again. Ninety per cent of inspectors said that reports are delivered within a month, and yet only 56% of providers agree. Nearly a quarter of providers have to wait rather too long than they should have to.

quantitative or qualitative?

We asked whether inspection reports should be either *quantitative* (based on clear, objective, measurable criteria) or *qualitative* (based on quality of life experience and outcomes) or a combination of both. All 30 inspectors who replied agreed that inspection reports should combine both quantitative and qualitative aspects. One hundred providers also agreed that both aspects should be included. However, seven providers felt reports should only be quantitative, and four thought reports should only be qualitative.

There was a very similar response to the question whether inspectors should make judgements or offer opinions (based on evidence) or whether they should just stick to facts which are indisputable or a combination of both. The judgements and facts combo was the favoured option: all 30 inspectors thought so, as did 99 providers (out of 111). Only eight providers thought that inspectors should stick to the facts alone, while four providers (probably misreading the question) thought inspectors should only make judgements.

providers' responses

Out of 105 replies only one provider said that they are not asked to comment on their inspection report. We also asked those who were asked to comment on their report how long they were given to make their comments. The 83 providers who gave a time (some of whom said they were unsure) did so as follows:

time given to reply to an inspection report	number	percentage
1 week	2	2%
10 days	3	4%
2 weeks	26	31%
2–3 weeks	9	11%
3 weeks	1	1%
4 weeks/1 month	35	41%
4–6 weeks	1	1%
6 weeks	1	1%
60 days	1	1%
others (see * below)	4	5%

*Four providers also replied with the following statements: 'no time given'; 'several weeks'; 'reasonable time'; and 'not stated'.

It seems to me that providers should have the same time to reply to an inspection report as it takes the unit to deliver it to them – with an agreed minimum amount of time. For me, there's just something fundamentally wrong that a report taking three months to arrive demands a response within three weeks.

what providers think of inspection

We gave providers a range of phrases to describe inspection reports. We asked them to tick all the ones that best described how they felt about their inspection reports. The replies from 115 providers are as follows:

Providers commented on inspection reports:

I don't always agree with their recommendations and I then tell them that. Sometimes the report is altered.

Not enough about the 'feel' of the home, sometimes very factual.

Recognition of improvements not always given.

No measure of quality of life. The best mark achievable is 'satisfactory'. No comments for best practice or excellence.

Inaccurate and careless – typed version not checked before sending.

Not writing subjective comments on reports.

A visit after the report is completed might be useful in some instances for some feedback about how some judgements might have been made.

One who gives a clear, concise and unbiased report with no personal opinions and who at all times maintains consistency and truth.

description of inspection reports	number	percentage
detailed and thorough	87	76%
too short	1	1%
clearly written	80	70%
good use of plain English	79	69%
poorly designed	11	10%
fair	57	50%
unreasonable	10	9%
too long	17	15%
about the right length	63	55%
too much jargon	13	11%
complicated language	7	6%
well designed	35	30%
sometimes unfair	42	37%
other (see * below)	7	6%

* Other descriptions given by providers were: 'not always factual'; 'some disagreement'; 'lack incentive'; 'lack understanding of clients'; 'subjective'; 'sometimes factually incorrect'; 'repetitive'. [If it's repetitive for the provider, think what it must be like for the poor inspector]

The clear message here is that providers are, in general, happier with inspection reports than I am. But that's me: in touch with the world, a barometer of the nation's thoughts. Most notable on the positive side is providers feel that reports are detailed and thorough, clearly written with a good use of plain English. However, significantly, only half of providers felt reports to be fair, with 37% experiencing a degree of unfairness.

I have had experience of reports written in a very scathing and unproductive manner.

Also significant is that only 30% of providers thought reports to be well designed. In the review below of inspection reports this is highlighted throughout. Inspection reports don't have to be slick but some thought should go into making them good to look at. For example, a great enemy to looking good is the question/answer approach.

SECTION 6 – CATERING FACILITIES

a) What are the arrangements for?

i) Breakfast
8.30 a.m. – 9 a.m. onwards in rooms or dining room.
ii) Lunch
12 p.m.
iii) Tea/Dinner
4.30 – 5 p.m.
iv) Supper
7.30 p.m. onwards
v) Additional refreshments
Early morning drink. Ongoing. Any drink on request.

Note: A sample menu of day of visit should be attached to this report, as should be menu sheets for two weeks.

This could easily be transformed:

6   Meals and Mealtimes

6.1 Mealtimes in the home are:

breakfast	8.30 – 9.00am
lunch	midday
tea	4.30 – 5.00pm
supper	7.30 onwards

6.2 Residents also get an early morning drink and are able to ask for a drink anytime. Meals are usually served in the dining room, but residents can also have meals in their bedrooms, particularly breakfast.

6.3 A copy of the menu served on the day of the inspection, along with menus for the last two weeks, are attached to the back of this report.

review of inspection reports

One provider, during the research for this book, noted sombrely that caring is more about covering your back these days. Sadly, from what I have seen, as far as inspection reports are concerned, we need to think more about covering our fronts also. Inspection report covers display a lack of creativity that is mind-numbing even by inspection unit standards. In this day and age, where the magazine culture rules, people expect sharp design and strong images. They don't just expect their attention to be grabbed, they expect it to be shaken up and down, pulverised and left for dead. So, how do inspection units go about this attention-mugging process? In a word, they don't. Is it really any wonder that uptake is low? Go on, look at the reports you write, receive or read: if you didn't have to read it – would you pick it up?

Below are four examples of inspection report covers. At least Solihull's looks like a cover. The other three represent, in my view, a

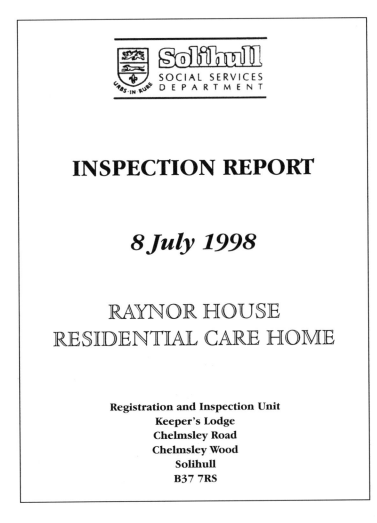

Wandsworth Borough Council – Inspection Report – Adult Residential Care Homes

WANDSWORTH BOROUGH COUNCIL
Social Services Department
Registration and Inspection Unit

Community Care Act 1990, Registered Homes Act 1984, Residential Care Homes Regulations 1984

Draft/Final Annual Inspection Report

Name of Home:

Address:

Telephone:

Client Category:

Registered Number of Places: **Date of Initial Registration:**

Registered Person(s) in Control:

Registered Care Manager:

Company/Organisation:
(if applicable)

Type of Inspection:

Date of Inspection: **Time of Inspection:**

Name of Inspecting Officer(s):

Name of Lay Assessor:

(I)
This inspection report is a public document and copies can be seen at:
- Careline Wandsworth Information Centre (reports for elderly persons homes only)
  0181 875 0500
- Welbeck House – Wandsworth High Street. Reception Area (all reports)
  0181 871 6316
- Wandsworth Pubic Libraries (reports for elderly persons homes only)
(II)
Copies of all reports are available from the Registration and Inspection Unit at the Town Hall, Wandsworth High Street, London SW18 2PU   Tel: 0181 871 6265
(III)
All registered Homes should make a copy of this report available to all residents, relatives and staff working at the home.
(IV)
Reports can be made available in large print for those who require them. Please ask the Registration and Inspection Unit on 0181 871 6265

Brigh

ANNUAL

TEL

Category of Care:

Numbers Registered:

Fees:

Owner:

Manager:

Date(s) of Inspection:

Time(s) of Inspection:

Name of Inspector:

Registrat
Hov
H

Tel: (0

---

common failing for units: covers that provide too much information, with the unit itself hogging the limelight rather than the home and the inspection. In contrast are the two inspection report covers used by Barking & Dagenham in 1997 – the adults homes inspection cover had colour photographs.

In 1998, the covers changed again to being a single photograph of a resident particular to each client group. The children's daycare inspection covers also changed – although this happened after I left. A competition was held for children to design the cover for each particular service: so, children with childminders would design the childminders report cover, children using a crèche would design the

DRAFT REPORT
(date)

ɔve

N REPORT

JO

ion Unit
ons
s

)50/I

2il Llawr   2nd Floor
Canolfan Victoria   Victoria Centre
Stryd Mostyn   Mostyn Street
Llandudno   Llandudno
LL30 2RP   LL30 2RP

Ffon/Tel   01492 574053

**UNED COFRESTRU AC ARCHWILIO
REGISTRATION AND INSPECTION UNIT**

REGISTERED HOMES ACT, 1984.   **FILE REF:** Forms\Repannin.Sam

Type of Report: Annual

Announced or Unannounced Inspection:

Name of Establishment:

Address:

Telephone Number:

Category:

Registered Numbers:

Person[s] in Control:

Manager:

Date and time of Visit:

Name of Visiting Officer:

Total number of pages:

This report may only be reproduced as a whole and may not be quoted
in part or in any abridged form for any public or statutory purpose.

Page 1

---

crèche cover, and so on. On top of this, the unit managed to get some excellent prizes donated by local businesses: including a computer and a professional keyboard. The unit also organised a prize giving party. Not only did this innovative thinking result in great designs for covers (one of the winning drawings was called 'The cat is cross') but the profile of inspection in the borough and the unit itself was raised through the whole process.

Anyway, onto the content of reports. When open reporting became a requirement for reports on nursing homes, the guidance (Local Authority Social Services Letter (98) 4), the government decided to append a proposed template for authorities to follow, describing it

as a 'step towards more consistent reports.' It is, in my view, a very big step backwards. The order of subjects and the design does little to help make reports accessible or lively. Admittedly, it does also say that the template 'is not intended to stifle unduly the many and varied examples of good inspection reporting practice which are in use.' However, this smacks of the 'let's not upset anyone by calling their reports crap' approach. But clearly they must think reports are crap – because if there was some good work out there, why didn't they use that? This template has precious little to commend it.

Even on a simple design front, the over-use of capital letters for words like Home, Residential and Nursing simply irritates. Distracting capital letters aside, why call section 2 'Summary of the Main Findings of this Inspection' when you can call it a 'summary'? Only bureaucrats and academics could draw up something so lacking in people: sections 4 and 5 are 'Environment' and 'Records, policies and administration'. Despite the latter thankfully shedding capital letters, things and bits of paper are given more credence than the poor people who live, work or visit these homes ... er, Homes, sorry.

Interestingly (used euphemistically for 'stupidly' in this case), section 6 'Complaints' precedes section 7's 'Services'. So we can find out what goes wrong with a service before we know what it is they provide. Don't get me wrong, complaints are important, but I do think they are sometimes pushed into your face too much. For example, if you walk into a social services reception and the first thing you see is a 'How To Complain' poster, it doesn't exactly inspire you with confidence about an organisation, now does it? Indeed, I'm reminded of someone telling me about a client they knew who went to a social services reception but gave up and left after being handed the 'how to complain', 'access to records', 'confidentiality', 'duty system' and 'equal opportunities' leaflets. They only went in to renew their bus pass.

We have to wait until section 8 (Management of Care) until we get to care planning or rather Care Planning (and even then it is listed below 'Admission process' and 'Discharge process') – which I consider to be central to the whole caring process. Interestingly it adds a bracketed afterthought – 'including involvement of users/relatives in care planning'. Why add this here? Shouldn't this be intrinsic throughout? Why is this not an issue for other sub-headings such as 'Choice', 'Suitability of equipment', 'Renewal of clothing', 'Menus etc' (whatever 'etc' is supposed to stand for), 'Key Worker system' and so on and on?

The section on Social Care trots in at number ten (of 12). While the preamble to the template says, quite rightly, that reports 'should include relevant comments of residents, relatives and other professionals throughout', there is no section set aside for residents to say what they think of the home.

Staffing finds itself at section 11, although there is nowhere set aside for inspectors to comment on the *quality* of care provided by staff, concentrating as it does on rotas, numbers, cover, training and supervision. It is important that homes have the correct number of staff, but I would have thought that the quality of staff was as important as the quantity. One of the categories in this section is called 'Relations with residents'. Now, I am not sure this is legal, let alone appropriate care practice. Also, residents, you will note, did not get a capital letter, thereby signalling to me, at least, that they are less important than the Home, Procedure Manual and Key Worker, which all command the max respect of a capital letter. It's more like capital punishment if you ask me.

In my view the template lacks clarity of thought, is bureaucratic (which is probably the same thing really) and unhelpful. If this is the model for the Care Commission, we're doomed.

However, the template holds no monopoly on bad design. **Islington** prefer a strange order to things also. For example, we get to know all about the residents' health. By page 8 we know how many of them have a colostomy, but we don't get to see what they have to say until page 40 (of 41). The terminable use of tick box or rather yes/no answers may be comprehensive but is hopelessly dull. Especially so, as it has a numbering system complexity that would cause open and flagrant sexual delight to that happy breed known as statisticians:

4a.5 is staff vacancies and turnover (only naturally in capital letters, bold and italic). Wow, what does this button do? Question 4a.4.2 (from a section headed '**4A. STAFFING** (Standard 4)' asks 'Is staff sickness a significant problem?' No, but your numbering system is, mate. Yes, we even have the market leading reference 4b.1.5.7. Now, that's class.

Wandsworth have a table of contents, or rather a **TABLE OF CONTENTS**, which although weakly designed does, praise be, list section 1 as 'User Views and Relatives Views'. However, sadly section 6 'Quality Of Life: Values' has but one page compared to the four set aside for section 7 'Physical Aspects Of The Home'. Their format highlights the negativity of inspection. Inspectors are asked to say whether each standard is met or not (always a bit arbitrary that – if 59 out of 60 bedrooms are fine but one has a wardrobe with a broken door, then the furniture standard has to be not met). They can only comment when something is not met: inspectors are instructed to 'Provide details if not met'. If it's met, say nowt.

The full bold, caps and underlining treatment is dished out for the section headings. Section 14 being 'provider feedback regarding quality of inspection team (You should include the Lay Assessor in this feedback report)' it helpfully adds in mostly lower case but holding down that bold key. Providers are given five areas to make known their feedback regarding the quality of the inspection team. These are: Planning of Inspection; Courtesy/ Punctuality/ Liaison; Conduct During Inspection; Application of Standards; and Clarity of Feedback/Requirements. I'm sorry but, for me, this smacks of the no-real-thought-needed school of monitoring. Perhaps they don't need to know what providers think, inspectors are professional after all.

However, I did like Wandsworth's idea to send out notices saying that the inspection has taken place, that the report is now available and where you can get a copy. While the heading of 'important notice' smacks a bit of self-importance, and the 'Please ask to see it for your information' is a touch desk-issued memorandum in style, the idea is a very good one.

Now here's a way to inspect. **Stirling**'s inspection reports are put together from visits made over the year. The report I saw was compiled from six visits made from February to December. It was also the biggest report I saw being a monster 47 pages plus cover. But 'resident's rights' from the contents page (the misplaced apostrophe is corrected later) in the actual report on page 5 becomes 'Standard 1: Residents' rights must be respected and promoted. These include the right to privacy, the right to be treated with dignity, the right to choose and the right to an independent lifestyle'. And all in bold and caps and in huge lettering, which is the most frightening thing you ever saw. I think the Stirling approach has a lot to commend it, although I worry – it's the catholic upbringing and the integral guilt that goes with that, I'm sorry – about an inspection visit in February not resulting in a report until December. However, at least it's planned that there is a 11 month wait for the report, unlike some other places. I could mention them but the publishers would like to sell at least ten copies of this book. I just wish their inspection reports could be less, well, ugly, frankly.

Kirklees (Huddersfield and a bit) and **North Yorkshire** share the same reporting approach. The reports concern themselves in the main with **SRs** (that's **S**tatutory **R**equirements, to me and thee). However, Kirklees have a summary at the start and look at the quality of life of residents in section 2 before hitting the meat of the SRs. In both units, inspectors are given freedom to comment after each of the 24 SRs (North Yorks) or 26SRs (Kirklees). As for interest and readability, I know that inspection reports aren't going to be exactly page-turning grippers, but count the crows, you've gotta give 'em a chance. After getting to SR3 (having already endured *multi-disciplinary assessment*, and the inspector *deeming* stuff), I was checking to see if the sun had passed the yardarm and reaching for the single malt. Pages and paragraphs are unnumbered, there's no contents page, and I didn't know what the inspector actually thought of the place until a **GENERAL COMMENTS** section after the comments following SR24.

I did enjoy the North Yorkshire disclaimer at the top of the page of the lay assessor's report (which, strangely, had no heading): 'The Lay Assessor may express views which reflect the independent nature of their involvement in the inspection process'. Nothing quite like keeping your distance.

The Royal Borough of **Kingston-upon-Thames** do not number paragraphs and you have to hunt out the page number on the foot of the page. They plough through their 32 standards, which confusingly are numbered differently in their standards manual, so we have standard 32 (15). It is standard 32 in the report but standard 15 in the 'Royal Borough's Manual'. Well that comment alone was enough to inflame all my republican sensibilities and wisely decided it was probably best to move on.

Vale of Glamorgan use a system of continuous paragraph numbering. So they don't stop off for a 2.1 or 5.3, they go straight through from 1 to 90. Their 'Content' page gives the range of paragraphs that each subject has, and not the page where to find it. So, 'Residents and their quality of life' could be found between '58 – 70'. Pleasingly the first thing you get to read is a 'summary of findings' which is a sentence giving you a flavour of what the inspector thought: 'This is a well run home with high standards of decor and cleanliness and where residents' needs are met on an individual basis in a homely atmosphere.' A bit stilted, perhaps, but to the point and you know that the inspector thinks this is a good home. This is followed by a summary of good practice. This is good, positive and encouraging. Then comes the summary of requirements and recommendations. Then the introduction. The order is kicking.

Unfortunately, 'Residents and their quality of life' tells us little about what residents have to say. It does tell us about how many residents there are, number of admissions and discharges (am I alone in disliking that word? – although I do love the story of a hospital social worker submitting copy for a leaflet they had wanted to call 'You and Your Discharge'), the age range of residents and the average length of stay (which considering it was a home for older people is perhaps a tad morbid). The report notes that 'Of the 26 residents in the home on the day of inspection, 19 were seen, 15 of whom were spoken with. Of the four not spoken with, one was reading in her room, one was sleeping in her room and two were sleeping in the lounge. Of the 15 spoken with, four were spoken with in private in their bedsitting rooms, four were spoken to as a group in the lounge, four were spoken to as a group in one conservatory, one was spoken with in another conservatory, one was spoken with in the hall and one was spoken to in the dining room.' And yet for all this detail, not one word is used to describe what they actually **said**. The next (and last) two paragraphs in this section 'Residents and their quality of life' remember, begin with the phrase 'The manager says...'

Cambridgeshire number their introduction 1.0. Why people resort to '*.0*' as a decimal place is beyond me. It's a computer nerd thing and has no place in intelligent society. Disappointingly, 'Quality of residential experience' is placed at section 9. Or, rather Section 9.0. What the inspector thinks about a home (well at least it's there) is left to the last section called 'Concluding Summary'.

The 'Proprietor/Manager comments on inspection report and inspection process, together with any suggestions for improvement' on the last page requires the home's manager to fill in the name of the home, the name of the registration and inspection manager and the date of inspection. It's going to be part of the final report so the questions need not really be asked. And how difficult can it be for the unit to fill these in even if the questions have to be asked? The copy I saw had the manager's response handwritten. Now, while on the one hand it is personal, it inevitably sits very poorly next to the ordered, typed inspector's report. The effect is to have the inspector seem professional and the provider amateurish. Or perhaps that's the idea. Many inspectors still hand write reports and get them typed up because they look better that way. Would it be impossible to have provider's responses typed up (unless, of course, they prefer to see their response handwritten).

In Barking & Dagenham, we offered all providers (including childminders) the choice to have their responses typed. This would be sent back to them by return of post for them to check and sign. Certainly it made more work for us, but the end result was very worthwhile. This was particularly so for childminders who let us know that having a detailed report, bound with a picture cover, and their responses typed, gave them a sense of pride in their work. They felt valued. And shouldn't that be a good thing?

Derbyshire lead with an introduction and then a summary, followed by a summary of recommendations. No summary of commendations, though. The quality standards that their reports say an inspector 'will be mindful of' are laid out at the back of the report. I could not quite work out why they weren't used as headings and with the inspectors comments underneath. Once again, the order of the standards is disappointing: management, buildings and catering, staffing, quality of care, and quality of life.

There is a page for the 'observations of owner/manager' (no other guidance). At the bottom of the page is a note in brackets: 'If this section is blank and/or no correspondence from the owner/manager is appended – then no observations/comments have been made'. I think it's really important to get the view of the provider. However, if they choose not to reply despite reminders then, quite rightly a report should be published with no comment. However, how this is handled may provoke a response next time. By putting in a statement that the inspection unit values responses but that this provider despite reminders (and put in details of how unit has tried to encourage a response) has chosen not to, can send a very serious message out to prospective residents and purchasers of care. Just a thought.

Liverpool sent in a copy of their report format (rather than an example report) and I only hope that their public reports are better photocopied or produced. Their format makes use of questions, yes/no boxes and boxes for comments. This means that the longer the question, the bigger the box for the yes/no and the comments. This in turn means that the sizes of the boxes are all different which is all somewhat less than handsome. Inevitably, as is the case when using a standard boxed approach, some of the questions do not require yes/no answers. For example, 'What training has taken place in the last twelve months?', 'How are staff recruited?', 'Available hours of domestic staff (total)? and 'How is food served/presented?'

Aberdeenshire win the contest for the smallest typeface used. Most units prefer, quite rightly, to use at least 12 point. I think Aberdeenshire use 10 point. It may save a tree here and there but if people don't read the reports because the print is so small, then the paper is wasted anyway. My advice over your print size, in keeping with my adopted local (Romford) lingo, is to *large* it. Also a lack of margin on the left and right hand side make it also very unappealing to the eye. No line of text should really average more than 15 words a line. Some of these went up to 22 words in a line (and this is with an unhealthy sprinkling of big words). Although just six pages long, they do use a summary of findings near the front – after the introduction. The sections for Part III (never use roman numerals – it's not big and it's not clever – stick to 1, 2, 3 and so on) 'Findings of Inspection' is divided into four parts: management systems, premises, staffing, and (once again bringing up the rear) care of residents.

East Dunbartonshire have a positive approach to the ordering of sections in their announced reports. They start off with introduction, background, beliefs and values (of the home), quality of care and support, quality of management, and quality of environment.

Requirements and recommendations are listed at the end. Their reports could benefit from including a summary and paragraph numbering. However, what I particularly liked was the use of an additional single page double-sided summary report. Its four excellent headings are 'the house', 'activities', 'food', and 'how does it feel to live here?'. There is also a box for 'highlights' (what the home does well) and one for 'room for development'. This is also, in the main, written in plainer English than the announced and unannounced reports. A recommendation from an unannounced report ran: 'Managers should continue to be alert to the need to maintain the dynamism of the service and, in particular, continue the recent developments in the outreach service based on a person centred approach.' The manager replied that this was not accepted as an appropriate recommendation. I'm with the manager on that one.

Commendably, **Poole** have put some thought into the look of their reports which are simply and attractively laid out. The fact that capital letters are for the most part rejected in favour of lower case letters, in my view, greatly adds to this. The reports include a summary which follows three sections – 'basic home's facts' (which actually reads that it is the *home* and not the *facts* that are basic), 'introduction' and 'brief description of the home'. While the report lists commendations (which is commendable in itself) each standard is judged to be either 'below standard', 'meets minimum standard' or 'of merit'. The 'meets minimum standard' judgement seems quite deflating to me as it reads like a provider has just scraped in. Perhaps dropping the word 'minimum' would help.

Impressively, Poole say in their reports that the aim of the inspection is to 'assess the quality of care and quality of life experienced by residents'. They then list the eight methods they use to do just that. Depressingly, seventh of the eight listed methods is 'speaking to residents' while 'inspecting the building' is second. Similarly, 'social care' is the seventh of the eight areas covered in the 'detailed findings of the report'. The numbering system could be neater (I always think it best to keep to one decimal place – 2.5, 3.2 – than moving into two decimal places: 5.8.10, 5.5.5) and the English plainer (we have 'the lay assessor's comments have been woven into the body of this report'; and they prefer 'There is a central heating system in each of the properties' to 'both homes are centrally heated') but overall, I think, one of the better inspection reports.

The most notable thing about the inspection reports of **Scottish Borders** is the cover. As a design, in common with far too many other units, it's no great shakes. But what I liked about it was the largest name on the cover (or the thing that grabs your attention first) is not the name of the authority, or inspection unit, or the words 'inspection report' or even the full, uncensored title of the 1984 Act, but the name of the home. How simple is that? There are other things to commend Scottish Borders reports, they are clean and neat, and at least 'records' is section 8 of 10. Section 3 is called 'residents' but restricts itself to telling us about residents and not what they think. This does happen, though, in section 6 'health and social care' and in the summary skulking at the back of the report at section 9. Scotland makes it to second base again.

A joint health and local authority report from **Walsall** opens well enough with a glossary. This could easily be a lot more detailed. It tells us what is meant by a requirement and a recommendation and explains what is meant by UKCC, ENB and NVQ. It offered no clue about 'monitoring of hot water outlets' (*taps* perhaps?). The report used an interesting tactic of placing any provider comment on the report not at the end of the report but at the relevant part of the report. I have previously done this but only where there was a significant dispute between the inspector and provider. An interesting idea, nonetheless.

However, once again what the residents have to say is some way through the business of the report. Section 5 is called 'Discussion with residents and relatives'. It is on page 14 of 18 and amounts to four sentences.

Brighton & Hove also have a glossary but have this at the back end of the report and overkill on the bold print. Their reports have three 'appendices' (lay assessor's comments; requirements and recommendations, and commendations) and two 'annexes' (glossary of terms and categories of care; and confidential section). Yup, beats me, too. Pleasingly, in explaining the process of inspection the reports note: 'In writing this report, the inspector has spoken with residents, interviewed staff and the person in charge of the home, looked at the accommodation and also the records kept.' This clearly puts people first and is to be commended. However, resident care is section 5 in the main report following accommodation. So we get to know about the appropriateness of the car parking facilities before we know what it might be like living in the home.

Staffordshire don't go for paragraph numbers – or page numbers come to that, which means the contents page is a bit ineffective to be honest. But they do have a preface. This preface takes great pains (which are shared by the reader, let me tell you) to explain that the report can only be a snapshot of life in the home as observed by the inspector at the time. Or, as the Staffs staff put it: 'It should be appreciated that these twice-yearly inspection visits to residential care homes, whether they be independent or local authority, are time-limited, and therefore within the resources and time available, inspections provide an opportunity to develop a 'snapshot' of the quality of care provided within a particular home and to evaluate – on the day of the inspection visit – whether the home continues to meet registration standards. As such the 'snapshot' and the resulting conclusions which are set out in this Inspection Report are based on detailed observations, systematic checks and discussions with staff, residents and others on the day of the inspection and therefore the findings of the Inspection Report should be regarded as relating to the situation in the Home at the time of the inspection.' Well, at least I spared you the bold and italics.

The summary is up near the front on page 7. This is the first nine section summary I think I've ever come across, including as it does a list of basic information, detailing bedrooms and shaft lifts alongside all the disabilities, illnesses, behavioural patterns and frailties of residents. The last section is 'Quality of Care/Life for Residents'. It is quite extraordinary given the quoted example from the preface, that they should look to save three words from this headed section of the summary. Replacing the '/' for 'and quality of' and calling it 'Quality of care *and quality of* life for residents' is just too long winded, I guess. The main report kicks off with a major use of '/': 'Buildings/ Facilities/Environment/Equipment'. Under each part of the main report is listed the 'core criteria' each of which the inspector has decide if it is 'satisfactory' (in which case a tick is given), a 'not applicable' or a more worrying 'see report'. This means that we need to read the section marked **'Comments Re Core Criteria:'**. The 40 page report is certainly comprehensive and as such understandably needs to have a bold capital lettered emboldened **'INSPECTION SERVICES'** footer just to remind us who is responsible for all this copyrighted © information.

Solihull have clearly put a lot of thought into their layout and design of report and it's certainly good and interesting to look at. It includes a long summary which runs to five pages. Summaries should be kept to no more than one side if possible. But it seems this summary is also issued as a separate report so it includes more information than it would need if was simply part of the full inspection report. Although why Solihull should call it an 'executive summary' when 'summary' does the trick, I'm not sure. Also, although five pages are devoted to the 'outcome from the current inspection' which is a 'quality audit on the rights of residents', there wasn't a reference to what the residents themselves had to say. The policy of calling the place a 'provision' rather than a 'home' ('description of provision', 'Name of Provision') seems unnecessarily pompous. They also fall into the trap of saying things without qualification or judgement. For example, the statement that 'All staff wear a uniform and name badge' made me ask, 'so is that good or bad – and if so – why?' Still, in terms of presentation Solihull impressed.

You have to wait until the conclusion (section 12 of – as you might expect – 12) before you can be sure what inspectors thought of a home in **Conwy**. The shape of the report would be so much better if this conclusion was dropped in favour of a summary at the start of the report. Likewise the section called 'promotion of individual' (which could do with *the* before *individual* as it could be read as an error: promotion of individual – what? – rights, tea cups, -ly wrapped sandwiches?). This charts at section 9 and could be a lot nearer the top. I was also intrigued by a sub-title in the staff section: 'support, supervision and discipline.' Whatever gets you through the night, I say. Whip crack-a-way.

some things to think about...

...for inspection reports

- take a look at your inspection report covers – be honest, would you pick it up?

- decide who it is you are writing reports for (better still consult about it) and target them appropriately. If you truly believe that residents are a target audience then write, design and distribute your reports accordingly.

- think seriously about the order in which you put your subjects. Put them in order of importance and then devote more time and space to the more important and less to the less important.

- keep capital letters, bold and italics to a minimum. Destroy your underlining button. Use a clear typeface (for example, Univers) and never drop below 12 point. Keep referencing to one decimal place.

- look to use a summary at the start of your report – and use it to summarise the findings of the report: make judgements.

- look to use a contents page, number your paragraphs and your pages.

- use plain English.

- think about using a glossary.

- look to commend as well as requiring and recommending.

- if reports are lengthy, think about also issuing a short summary report (four sides at the most) which also tells readers how to get a copy of the full report if they want to see it.

- oh, and **never** call basic information 'principally static information'.

chapter 7 – conclusion

This probably sounds like I'm very anti-inspection! In fact I fully support the need for inspection in order to protect vulnerable adults/children. I just don't understand why it has to be such a combative process where it feels that the Inspection Dept is always right.

manager of a voluntary home

I feel I have had a good relationship with inspection officers. They have always assisted me by providing information and material if needed. They have even assisted me to push my organisation into providing more resources.

manager of a voluntary home

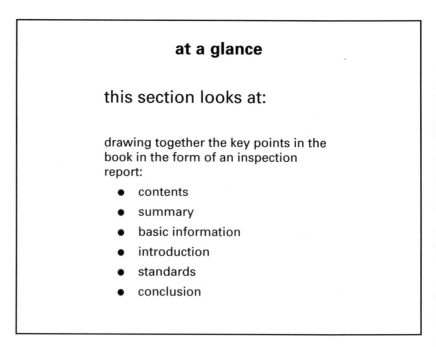

at a glance

this section looks at:

drawing together the key points in the book in the form of an inspection report:

- contents
- summary
- basic information
- introduction
- standards
- conclusion

contents

summary

This inspection looked at the effectiveness of the inspection process as seen through the eyes of inspectors and providers (the inspected). Its main finding is that while inspection protects and helps to improve services, there are many ways in which it can itself improve.

People should be at the heart of inspection but this is not necessarily the case. Residents, relatives and staff outside of management appear to form a very little part of the inspection process. Too much time is taken up with managers, paperwork and checking buildings and too little on the people who live, visit and work in them.

Our findings show that the effective inspector is the one who is approachable, human, supportive, respected and respectful, and positive in commending good practice as well as pulling up homes for shortfalls or recommending improvements.

There is a great variety between units as to what happens before an inspection. Some units require lots of information, others none at all. Where there are questionnaires sent out to individuals (residents, relatives, staff or other interested people) only some of these seem targeted for their audience. There also seemed to be some confusion as to why units should ask for such information, either because it is not clear why it is required or because it is simply asked for again at the inspection.

Inspection reports were too often poorly designed, lacking in judgements and dull. Reports should be written in plain English and some thought on the purpose of reports, and how they should be designed to achieve that purpose, needs to happen.

Nevertheless, on the whole, providers were satisfied with the way inspectors conducted themselves and with inspection processes.

principally static information

name	Inspection
address	United Kingdom, Europe, The World, The Universe, CV4 1AV
owner	C.A. Recommission (registration pending)
person in control	Rt Hon Francis 'Dobbo' Dobson (at time of inspection) – now Rt Hon Alan 'Alan' Milburn
certificate displayed	Dobbo's third prize in the parents egg and spoon race 1987 (but disqualified for eating the egg)
maximum number	no such thing as a maximum number – it's a swizz, it's like an all-day breakfast or a non-stop flight – they don't exist.
date of registration	1984 (amended in 1991)
date of inspection	March – September 1999
inspector	Graham Hopkins
type of inspection	well and truly announced
category of resonance	thunderous
reason for inspection	the above profession was inspected as required by Russell House Publishing Ltd, and section 17 (4) of the author's contract. The inspection was carried out using an inspection questionnaire for providers, inspectors and heads of inspection. The inspector also visited five inspection units interviewing the management and inspectors. Both inspector and the lay assessor visited homes and chatted to residents, staff and management.
number of admissions last year	just one. The author admitted to atrocious deadline meeting – so much for this book being out by September.

introduction

This report is based on fieldwork visits to five inspection units, which included meeting and interviewing residents in homes, providers of services, inspectors and unit management. Questionnaires were also received from providers, inspectors and heads of inspection units. It has also been based on the experience, ideas and beliefs of the author as both inspector and head of unit.

This report, by its very nature, is but a snapshot in the life of inspection, inspectors and the inspected.

the standards

inspectors

---

standard 1: inspectors

Inspectors should be approachable, warm, friendly, pleasant, human, polite, assertive, firm, calm, quiet, realistic, compassionate, caring, supportive, enabling, developing, encouraging, helpful, constructive, practical, respectful, respected, credible, confident, consistent, dynamic, efficient, empathic, enthusiastic, experienced, fair, flexible, honest, informative, intelligent, interested, knowledgeable, informed, a listener, objective, non-judgemental, open-minded, presentable, professional, qualified, sensitive, skilled, straightforward, thorough, trusting, understanding, reasonable, and have good inter-personal skills, memory, sense of humour, common sense and communication skills.

I feel really very happy with the inspectors we have had, and have always felt they are approachable and helpful. manager of a private home	*More approachable. More realistic. Constructive criticism not destructive. Have experience of working in a home. Less of a superior attitude. Act more as a colleague. Have more of an advisory role.* manager of a private home

1.1   This standard was drawn from comments made by providers during this inspection. Some providers are very happy with their inspectors, working in partnership with them and speaking highly of their manner, knowledge and support. When asked what makes for an ideal inspector, an owner/manager said 'The one I have now!' Similarly a manager of a voluntary home said the 'one we have comes pretty close.'

1.2 When asked how they thought their inspectors could improve
      some providers believed that would be hard to imagine. 'My
      inspector needs no improvement,' said one owner/manager.
      Another owner/manager agreed: 'As far as I am concerned my
      inspection officer is helpful. The team at the Registration and
      Inspection Unit are helpful, approachable and understanding. I
      have no complaints. I feel it would be difficult to find much
      room for improvement.' A manager of a private home also
      reported positively: 'I have worked in the nursing home sector
      since 1991. In that time there have been a few different
      inspectors who in my opinion carried out their duties
      thoroughly without being intrusive into the normal day to day
      events in the home. I have always felt that if I needed support or
      advice on any issue I could approach them and discuss this with
      them.' This is, of course, encouraging. Some other thoughts are
      boxed below.

Have always found [my inspectors] helpful. manager of a voluntary home	*Mine is excellent – always ready with advice and support at the end of a phone.* manager of a voluntary home
The present inspector is both professional, fair and friendly. manager of a private home	*I have enjoyed the inspections which I have experienced as a manager. I have had no problems or suggestions for change.* manager of a private home

1.3 However, not all providers felt this positively about their
      inspectors. Some providers thought there was room for
      improvement. These suggestions centred around
      approachability and flexibility. Providers strongly believe that
      the most important quality an inspector can have is
      approachability. Someone that they can turn to for help,
      support, guidance or discussion: a fellow human being and not
      a dictatorial, dyed-in-the-wool by-the-book bureaucrat. Some
      providers told us:

Some should learn how to carry their authority better. Often they can present as uncaring of home's difficulties and only interested in assessing whether standards are met or not. manager of a voluntary home	*By retaining a friendly, cheerful approach. I appreciate the need to be authoritative. After all, I am a manager but this approach should not be the premise of the relationship. The officers should not approach from a premise of suspicion.* manager of a voluntary home
Should have an informal, approachable manner to all. a provider	*To be friendly and understanding towards all concerned.* manager of a voluntary home
Be flexible. Be approachable. manager of a council home	*Be more approachable.* a provider
More approachable. Able to compromise. Not dictatorial. See others' points of view. owner/manager	*Inspectors should be more approachable.* owner/manager
Attitude. I feel inspectors, especially new ones, tend to be power mad. They come into your home and expect everything to change, they are not happy with anything you do despite all records etc meeting last inspector's criteria. In all they baffle me. They usually are not consistent so no proper 'standard' is ever met. manager of a private home	

Recommendation 1: inspectors should be seen as approachable, supportive and human.

1.4 Some providers felt that inspectors are, at times, too inflexible. They feel this stance flies in the face of the individuality not only of residents but of different homes and different client groups also. As a manager of a voluntary home said: 'We are always trying to respect residents' individuality and then inspection expects a uniform type of programme.' An owner/manager said that inspectors 'should be open to other people's views and opinions. [They] tend to be arrogant in that they always think they're right (e.g. they don't think uniforms are a good idea – but most clients and relatives do).' Some things will undoubtedly be uniform but these are mostly restricted to building requirements. Other uniform requirements such as care plans, aims and objectives can and should be individualised for each home. Some other thoughts from providers are boxed below.

Inspectors do not realise that no two homes are the same. owner/manager	*To be straight but realise that all things cannot be dealt with 'by the book'. To acknowledge that staff know residents better than them and that residents are individuals and therefore cannot be 'what's best for one is best for all'.* owner/manager
To make sure that all the recommendations do not apply to all homes as it depends on the clients in the home. All homes are different in some way. They should fully understand the home they visit. manager of a private home	*Inspectors in their training should spend a few days at anytime in the homes they inspect, to have a better understanding of the clients, staff and home and how some things work for some and not for others.* manager of a private home

It does look as though inspectors have their own ideals and we all have to conform within these ideals. This does not allow for the freedom of choice for the individual who requires care but wishes to be able to maintain their values from within residential care, if all homes were exactly the same. So – to be more flexible and open-minded when inspecting establishments.
manager of a private home

Residents need to feel valued. Standards and regulation are necessary but we need to provide a 'home' for people, therefore it is necessary not to be regimented or controlling for the sake of keeping the inspectors happy.
owner/manager

Recommendation 2: inspectors should consider each home on its individual merits, particularly when assessing the quality of care.

1.5   Some providers thought, surely rightly, that better relationships between the inspectors and the inspected can benefit both sides and, more importantly, the residents. An owner/manager said: 'There should not be a "them and us" attitude on both sides as we are trying to complement each other's work.' A manager of a council home felt that an inspector's supportive role should outgun their policing role: 'Some inspectors feel they have a policing role, which is unhelpful. Their role should be to enable owner/managers to look at what they are doing and how they could do it better.' Finally, in this section, a provider pleads with inspectors to give careful consideration about the impact of what they say and do: 'Many have their opinion of how things should be. Sometimes they need to look at the impact of what they are saying either the impact on the user or sometimes effect on staff!'

providers

standard 2: providers

Providers should be patient, understanding, tolerant, open-minded, respectful, informed, forward thinking, committed, supportive, respected, welcoming, warm, imaginative, energetic, conscientious, responsible, analytical, sensitive, experienced, humble, kind, dedicated, co-operative, well rounded individuals, hard working, careful, calm, compassionate, caring, professional, empathic, sharing, good listeners and be good communicators with a sense of humour.

In our opinion, our inspectors have worked extremely hard to forge good working relationships with service providers within our borough. owner/manager	*Realise most of us are trying our very best in sometimes very difficult circumstances and tight budgets.* manager of a council home

2.1 This standard was drawn from comments made by inspectors during this inspection. Some of the qualities required differ from those required of inspectors above, most notably being forward thinking, imaginative and humble. Not bad qualities for inspectors either. Caring for people can be (should be?) a fairly humbling one.

2.2 Some providers treat inspection as an unwelcome intrusion, some believe it to be essential but could be more informal and positive, but many see it as positive, helping them to develop and improve services. As one owner said: 'More openness is needed between us.' A manager of a private home agreed: 'Remember we are working with people! Have better communication skills. Build up relationships with providers so we work together.' As did another: 'Remember that partnerships work best and we are all professional people doing a professional job.'

2.3 Many providers believe that inspection is something to be embraced and not feared. As an owner/manager said: 'I feel that in general home owners should not dread inspectors (unless they have something to hide) but use them as a guide to whether they are offering a good service, and how to improve it if need be.' A manager of a private home added: 'A registration visit should be a "working together" for the benefit of our residents, with them giving us guidance where we may be failing. It should not leave us feeling it was a negative experience.'

2.4 Indeed, many providers believe inspection has helped them move on and improve services. 'I do not consider, said a manager of a private home, 'that the inspectors in this area can improve the way they go about their work. We have excellent communications between the inspectors and ourselves and they are always willing to discuss any matter at any time outwith inspection visits.' A manager of a council home agreed: 'I cannot fault the inspectors I have come into contact with over the past few years. I have moved forward with the experience and I know that the service has.'

2.5 Providers described the frustration and the rewards that went hand-in-hand with a job that is very hard work, often demanding and rarely as financially lucrative as popular opinion may well have it. Indeed, many commented on the quality of services expected by local authority contracts sections while turning the screw on fees. An owner/manager reported how difficult it is 'to know how some providers can provide a really good environment for residents when the majority of their clients are funded by Social Services to inadequate amounts.'

quality of pre-inspection

standard 3: quality standards

Standards used to inspect against should be consulted on widely, be clear, specific and include the quality of life experienced by residents living in a home.

Standards should fit the needs of the people not vice versa. manager of a private home	*Inspection needs to be about standards which are set on an even playing field. They need to be about standards not down to individual interpretations, we shouldn't be inspected on whims but on standards.* chief executive of voluntary organisation

Work in a home from time to time. To understand changes in clients to enable a more realistic approach to standards. Listen to staff more closely. Meet with people from all sides of the business to hear their views to get an overview of their local problems recruiting staff, placements etc.
owner/manager

3.1 Just as the draft of this book is completed, the government issued the proposed national standards for homes for older people. On the whole, they seem quite good. Although pleasing to note the order of the ten sections (the section *The Rights of Residents* is second and the *Physical Environment* is ninth) there does seem to be very little on the quality of life experienced by residents. As to be expected the controversy will be over the baselines for room sizes and single rooms which will cost money.

3.2 However, just to add to the debate, providers have said in the course of the book's research that standards should be clear and not open to interpretation and preferably should be specific to different client groups. The national standards may well achieve this, but they will not, I'm sure, be the answer everyone seems to imagine they will be.

standard 4: questionnaires

All pre-inspection questionnaires, if used at all, be kept to a minimum and be designed to help the inspection run more efficiently.

4.1 The disparity among inspection units is alarming – even by inspection unit standards. Some units have their heads so far into the sand of thoroughness that they despatch paper out before (sorry, prior to) inspections which could have added a whole new west wing to Tarzan's summer retreat. It would surprise little to learn that they may have never sat down and asked themselves (looking-into-mirrors time, folks) *why*? On the other vine, some units have dispensed totally with pre-inspection questionnaires.

4.2 The only value of a pre-inspection questionnaire is to save inspectors' time at the inspection finding out stuff that they could have (and trust) beforehand. Admittedly, there is the by-product of giving pointers about what to ask about at an inspection. But, I ask you, should an inspector ever be stuck for things to ask? The telling feature is that 48% of providers said that inspectors ask the same questions again, anyway. Too much information is sought by some inspection units. If any information isn't going to make it into the final report (for reasons other than confidentiality), then why ask for it?

Recommendation 3: only ask for information before an inspection that is relevant, used and which will help free up time during the inspection.

standard 5: encouraging interest

The inspection unit advertises the inspection in a way that encourages residents, relatives, staff and other interested people to take part. Questionnaires aimed at residents, relatives, staff and others should be targeted to their needs and be designed to interest them enough, so that they want to have their say.

> *I feel that pre and post inspection meetings between the inspectors and the whole staff team would be a good thing. This could be used as a means of introducing themselves to one another and also for inspectors to impress the importance of inspections as a part of the caring process upon staff.*
>
> manager of a council home

5.1 It was evident that some inspection units invest little in time and less in money in advertising inspections. Bland, black and white A4 sheets are served up as posters. Hardly the stuff to capture passing interest, let alone the imagination. Pre-inspection questionnaires for residents, relatives, staff, and other interested people also appear to be surprisingly underused. The net result might well be that the only people interested in inspection are the inspector and the manager. But perhaps that's how they like it. Inspectors spend so little time in a home over the course of a year they must surely value all the help they can get. Some organisations self-inspect or have quality audits. These would also be helpful for the inspector to see before an inspection. Indeed, a manager of a voluntary home suggested requesting 'copies of providers' internal quality audits' as a way of improving the inspection process.

5.2 However, some units have clearly made good headway. Some units use advocates to help residents prepare for inspections. Some inspectors visit homes to explain the process. Some have posters, leaflets and other interesting material aimed at different client groups. Units should always be on the look out for ways to improve the range, quantity and, ultimately, quality of information from others who, in the main, will know more about the home than any inspector. A manager of a council children's home exposes the lack of thought and consultation that has gone on: 'I feel that staff would probably like to discuss the home in a more relaxed setting. Maybe they should have the opportunity to complete questionnaires prior to visit.' In answering how inspections could be improved a manager of a voluntary home said 'Questionnaires for residents.' Neither of these are likely to be hot new products in the inspection innovations catalogue, and yet we're in danger of crediting them as good practice when, in reality, we ought to consider it bog standard practice.

Recommendation 4: units should think about how best to advertise inspections, look to include all interested people, and target questionnaires and information for different people.

quality of inspection process

standard 6: length of inspection

Inspections should last as long as they need to with an agreed minimum time set aside.

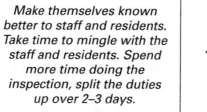

Make themselves known better to staff and residents. Take time to mingle with the staff and residents. Spend more time doing the inspection, split the duties up over 2–3 days.

owner/manager

A difficult job. Could it be shorter than 8–9 hours?

manager of a private home

6.1 The time taken to complete an inspection is impossible to prescribe. It just needs to take as long as it needs. However, there should be an agreed minimum time that any type of inspection should take. From our research, the average length of an announced inspection is seven hours and 40 minutes and an unannounced inspection is just short of four hours.

6.2 The length of time allotted to an inspection could be affected by workload or risk assessments made on homes – where 'better' homes receive less inspection time. However, by no means are providers all for shorter inspections. As one council home manager said 'Inspections are now faster – more cramped – so some things might go unnoticed! I would welcome going back to longer inspections as it gave more room to discuss issues and makes the whole process more personal.'

6.3 Also, very importantly, longer inspections mean more time to spend with residents. It seems that current inspection practice is to rate time with the manager, buildings and records higher than that spent with residents. So, lay assessors are deployed to 'take care' of this aspect of inspection. As standard seven next will look at, that's all upside down. And providers agree. An owner/manager suggested the inspection process could improve if inspectors 'make themselves known better to staff and residents. Take time to mingle with the staff and residents. Spend more time doing the inspection, split the duties up over

2–3 days.' A manager of a private home agrees: 'More time spent in the home on announced visits to enable more time to be spent with residents.' The manager of a voluntary home suggests 'More short visits during which the staff and residents will become familiar with them and would make the announced visit less intimidating.'

Recommendation 5: inspection should take as long as necessary but should always include enough time to spend effectively with residents.

standard 7: approach to inspection

Inspectors should, unless otherwise necessary, approach inspections in a relaxed, informal, supportive manner, looking to be as positive as possible.

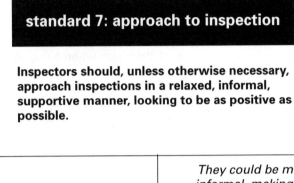

We have been fortunate in being inspected in a very positive manner resulting in inspectors being viewed as supportive and non-threatening by clients and staff. Managers have been invited to seminars to meet with members of the inspection unit and to discuss all areas of the inspection process. This has been very positive and successful. manager of a voluntary home	*They could be more informal, making the inspection less stressful.* owner/manager
	They only focus on negative aspects and never praise, where praise may be due. owner/manager
	By appearing to be approachable and making themselves available when the provider has a query, also by providing positive feedback not just negative. manager of a voluntary home

7.1 The approachability of inspectors is very important to providers. It's something that is appreciated when it happens and is yearned for when it doesn't. Providers are seemingly in no doubt as to the need for inspection as part of a regulatory regime but strongly feel that inspection could be improved if it was more informal, human and positive. An inspection, as this book has shown or perhaps, more accurately, reiterated, is a tense and anxious time for management, staff and, indeed, residents. It's no fun being watched while you work or live. The message is clear, unless serious enforcement work is involved, the more approachable the inspector, the more effective the inspection. The inspector, for example, sharing a fag break with a care assistant is more likely to produce information than a contrived interview. It's human nature. And the nature of inspection needs to be human.

7.2 An owner/manager's recommendation for an improvement in the inspection process is stunningly simple: 'They should be a little more relaxed and understanding when they arrive on an unannounced visit and thus put the home at ease. A few simple words of comfort does wonders.' A manager of a voluntary home also took up the theme of unease, asking inspectors to be 'understanding and supportive' and asks that 'nerves of staff on inspection days to be better understood, [as] staff do not always work their best when being observed.' Other comments were:

We have experienced positive and supportive inspection and the service provided at present meets the needs of organisation, staff and clients. Re-introduction of a mental health discussion forum via the Inspection Unit would be an improvement as it has lapsed over the last two years and had been an ideal way of consulting service providers and service users in the past. manager of a voluntary home	*Be supportive. Give constructive criticism with practical advice. Involve all the staff to promote a positive liaison rather than a threatening role, to assist in motivation with praise as well as criticism. Often staff regard an inspector as a threat and do not always perform at their best. Be a resource for information and guidance. Give clear directives.* manager of a private home
Thinking they are policing and being autocratic. chief executive of voluntary organisation *Our inspectors always explain why they think something should change.* manage of a private home	*They could maintain more contact so that they do not 'swoop' once a year like an avenging angel – this would in no way undermine their role - but would assist with understanding of both people's working frameworks.* a provider

7.3 As well as being approachable, providers were also asking inspectors to be more positive. There is a feeling that inspectors only look for things going wrong rather than commending things going well. Part of this negativity is rooted in the images conjured up by the word *inspection*: checking up on, catching out. Once again, where positive work is highlighted by inspectors, this is appreciated. But clearly a positive approach isn't favoured by all units or inspectors. This is concerning. A real feeling remains that inspectors have but one task: to hunt out bad practice. This is, necessarily, part of the job. Providers said that they felt that if inspectors didn't find something wrong then they weren't doing their jobs properly. Or as one provider said inspectors must find something 'to justify their existence'. For this reason, some providers reported leaving things out for the inspector to find.

7.4 One provider asked inspectors to be 'more supportive rather than critical of work providers do.' A manager of a voluntary home thought inspectors in a unique position to be able to pass on good practice seen elsewhere: 'Given the range of their experiences and their knowledge of examples of best practice, inspectors could guide providers towards evidence of those best practices in order for them to be shared.' Had I stayed on at Barking & Dagenham, I intended to publish examples of the best, new and innovative practice our inspectors had come across in the year leading up to the inspection unit's next annual report. An idea, incidentally, that I take no credit for as it came from providers at the unit's annual conference *Making the most of inspection*.

7.5 Other comments by providers on being positive were:

Not all inspectors are unfair. Some can be difficult. This can lead to confrontation making things difficult. The inspector could improve this by giving credit when it is due. Not looking for something to complain about if it is not the case. Sometimes even making fair recommendations. Having knowledge and understanding of care housing, and not judging all services as the same. manager of a voluntary home	*Treat you as a colleague, a professional person. Realise it's a difficult job and give credit where credit is due. Don't come in initially telling you all the things you are doing wrong. Lead with the carrot and not the stick. Don't stare at care staff waiting for them to make a mistake. Don't pick up every little error as a huge problem that needs to be solved.* owner/manager

Focus more on positive achievements.

manager of a council home

Could improve on the general approach to providers and not be over powering.

owner/manager

Two tiers: one an informal, helpful – if serious insurmountable problems occur a policing tier to enforce breaches of serious nature.

owner/manager

My experience of being inspected has been very positive.

manager of a council home

By not having to find something to criticise when you both know that it is petty.

owner/manager

I feel that it is most important that there is as little disruption to services as is possible (after all our units are young people's homes) and although I fully understand and agree that inspections have to be carried out they should be informal and friendly – lessening the chances of both young people and staff feeling threatened.

manager of a council home

They need to take a positive not negative attitude and make suggestions for changes in a non-accusatory tone of voice. They are meant to help improve facilities and care for residents and work with proprietors to achieve these aims and try not to cause a negative attitude or friction. They should be non-threatening, yet firm in any requirements that are needed to achieve or maintain standards. They need to remember they are 'guests' as well as inspectors in the home.

a provider

Recommendation 6: inspection should be approached in an informal, human and positive way with inspectors looking to relax the home and commend good practice where it is seen.

standard 8: people first

Inspectors should put people first and spend as much time as possible with the people who live in homes. They should look to include, wherever possible, relatives, advocates and representatives of residents and as many of the home's care and support staff as possible.

Spend much more time dealing with people rather than filling in forms and paperwork. Talk to many more of the staff and residents. assistant manager of a council home	*The flexibility to concentrate on the quality of care rather than just the premises and a 'tape measure' approach.* owner/manager
Far too long going over written information, policies etc. Rather than looking at hands-on care being delivered. a provider	

8.1 The picture painted from our research (and backed up by the department of health's August 1999 summary of the inspection of 22 inspection units *Better Regulation Now!*) is that apart from the manager, people play a small role in the inspection process. An emphasis on being office-based with records and management means that actual observation of care practice and spending time with residents, relatives and non-management staff are given a low priority. Many units rely on lay assessors to do the 'people' bit. People must stop being just a 'bit' and be at the core of it all. A manager of a voluntary home suggested speaking to 'residents at the start of an inspection rather than at the end' would be a good way to improve inspections. It would be a start.

8.2 Spending more time speaking to residents and observing the home at work are seen by many providers to be more worthwhile indicators of good care rather than paperwork. Make no mistake, records are important and must be kept and managers will simply have to accept (and hopefully understand why) that is so. However, inspectors must widen the base of evidence. Observations and the experience of people living, visiting and working in a home are not the fancy decorations on or even the cream of an inspection cake made of paperwork and building: they are the very sponge of it all – they make up most of it.

8.3 A manager of a private home said that inspection 'is a difficult but very necessary job. [Inspectors] need to be able to see if the residents are being well cared for, well fed, comfortable and happy. They should be able to put less emphasis on certificates for various services and paper proof of standards and sense for themselves if the object of the exercise is being achieved.' A manager of a voluntary home agrees: 'Try to treat the inspection as more of a positive experience than an exercise in what the home might not have in the way of bits of paper.' A council home manager had the good, if perhaps impractical, idea that inspectors 'should introduce themselves to residents' before residents are admitted into a home. Although impossible to achieve (although given some inspector workloads I am aware of, perhaps not so impossible after all) the point is pertinent: it's the residents that inspectors ought to know.

8.4 Other providers' comments are boxed below.

Be more 'friendly' towards clients/relatives. *Sit with residents.* manager of a council home	*They should listen to the service users and accept that what the elderly really want not what they think they should have.* a provider
Spend more time with staff and relatives. manager of a voluntary home	
There are other ways to measure service quality other than inspecting records. manager of a voluntary home	*Inspectors should be seen as a tool to improve standards and more as a support to managers. Inspectors should have more time to spend with staff at all levels.* manager of a council home
There could be more contact with us, ie more than two visits a year. Some inspectors could have better communication skills and should take/be given more time to get to know their [homes]. manager of a council home	*I do not understand why inspectors do not spend more time with service users. I thought it was their home – not mine.* owner/manager

> *Inspection officers should inform staff of how they can assist an organisation and its staff. Inspection Officers have improved the quality of lives of tenants and staff by listening to them and stipulating particular requirements in their reports.*
>
> manager of a voluntary home

Recommendation 7: inspections should put people first. This means spending appropriate times with residents, relatives, all staff and other people interested in the home.

quality of post-inspection

standard 9: inspection reports

Inspection reports should be clear, readable and understandable, having in mind the needs of different audiences, and are available to the public. Providers should be given a chance to include their comments.

Often after an inspection a verbal report is given which often is very constructive, but the written report is totally different and often petty. owner/manager	*Not to be disillusioned as an owner if the report is not perfect (it never is); do not expect merits, even if you have the necessary required, it will still only be satisfactory.* owner/manager

9.1 Inspection units report a disappointingly small uptake of reports by the public. This may well be because people do not know that reports exist or where to get them. But it might just be because inspection reports are designed and written in a way that simply sends the public running scared. And it's not just the public. One provider suggested a way to improve the inspection process would be if inspectors explained 'what information they need in simple terms not jargon.' If people who work in the profession are bamboozled by the language what chance the public? With only a couple of exceptions, the research on inspection reports found them to be poorly designed, unclear and dull. The need for plainer English and a greater use of summaries and some thought into livening up the look of reports is greatly needed. Inspection units should remember that they are in the communications business: so start thinking about how best to communicate. Also, and again with only a couple of exceptions, little thought, time or money has been given to find ways to make reports meaningful to residents: the reason we all inspect in the first place. And that's a good place to put them: first.

> *Registration and Inspection need to balance reports. What would residents feel if only the negatives are reported?*
>
> manager of a voluntary home

Recommendation 8: inspection reports should be well designed, written in plain English and in forms that are helpful, understandable and meaningful to all those whom they are targeted at.

conclusion

How can inspection be improved?

In the past months we have seen various improvements in inspection procedures, and I feel the process is clear, defined, fair and useful. I cannot see any ways in which things could be better at present. Our inspectors are always available for advice and give a good service in the time allowed.

owner of a private home

By giving advice; admitting when wrong or mistaken. When a dispute arises 'my opinion' not good enough – everyone's opinion matters and should be taken into consideration. Should be able to judge without punishing. Being more realistic – approachable – not to be dreaded even when you know you are doing everything as it should be. One error is a non-compliance!!! Even when put right.

owner/manager

Perhaps we are lucky, but we have a very good relationship with inspectors and feel to criticise them would be unfair. general manager of a private home	*Try to recognise the valuable service that providers offer, the large number of employees and the contribution to the local, often fairly remote, community.* manager of a private home
By continuing to be a respected, valued separated service. manager of a council home	
Having only met professional, knowledgeable people who act accordingly throughout any inspection, I find this a very difficult question to answer. manager of a council home	*By not being intimidating, more supportive – displaying a caring attitude.* manager of a private home

Inspection is essential. It is the best way we have to help protect people who need others to help them. But it should also be a positive experience for all. It should help homes develop and improve. And to do this, inspection itself must keep looking to improve. It should put people at its heart. It should find ways to involve people effectively in the process. It should find ways to report findings in a way that interests and affects people. For by improving the inspection process the effect will be to improve the quality of life of those people who matter most: the people who live in homes.

appendix 1

It's always seemed fair to me that if inspectors inspect homes against agreed quality standards then the homes should have standards against which to judge the effectiveness of inspection. Following an inspection conference in 1997, Barking & Dagenham published standards for providers to do just that. These standards are reprinted below.

In researching this book, we asked providers if they already had any standards against which to judge the inspection process. Out of 116 that replied, 14 said they had, 12 were unsure and 90 said no they hadn't. Of those who were unsure and hadn't got any standards (of inspection, that is), seven remained unsure, three said no, and 77 (five didn't answer) said yes, they thought standards for the inspection process would be a good idea. Indeed one provider said it would be useful to have 'a guide to inspection and what to expect etc clearly written for new, basic grade staff and residents to explain what will happen and to reassure/explain why.'

standards for the inspection process
general standards

standard 1   What we believe in and what we do

We will make public a clear, user-friendly guide to the work of our inspection unit. It will say exactly what it is we believe in. And, it will make clear our responsibilities and how we intend to carry them out.

standard 2   How often we will inspect

We will inspect all residential care homes, day centres for adults and children's daycare services at least twice a year, one of which will be unannounced. Some services will receive at least two unannounced inspections as well as their announced inspection.

Childminders and homecare service providers will be inspected at least once a year. This will be announced.

standard 3   Setting standards

We will apply standards, which have been consulted upon and agreed, that are specific to the type of service provided and the client group that use that service. We will apply these standards fairly to all providers, without fear or favour.

standard 4   Our inspectors

We will only offer contracts to inspectors who are experienced in and knowledgeable about the services inspected or inspection or, preferably, both. They will have the skills to carry out their work effectively. They will usually also be qualified in social care.

Our inspectors will reflect the range of services inspected and the make-up of the borough. For example, we will look to recruit about 10% of our inspectors from ethnic minority groups and about 5% with some degree of disability. Any specialised services will be inspected by people who closely relate to the people who use those services. For example, if there was a children's home specialising in care for young black women we would look to recruit a black woman inspector specifically for that inspection.

standard 5   Working with others

We will always try to work together with Health Authority inspection unit, Havering Social Services Inspection unit and other local units.

before the inspection

---

standard 6   Setting the date of your inspection

You will be informed of the date of your main announced inspection as early on in the year as possible. However, we will always try to give you at least a month's notice.

standard 7   Sending out your pre-inspection pack

You will receive your pre-inspection pack at least one month before your inspection. However, we will try to make sure you get it about six weeks before.

Your pre-inspection pack will include:
- cover note

- poster advertising the inspection
- pre-inspection questionnaire
- questionnaires for residents and clients
- questionnaires for other interested people
- information for minority language speakers
- prepaid envelopes

Your pre-inspection questionnaire will be:
- as short as possible; and
- relevant to your particular service.

standard 8   Advocacy

We will look to develop the role of advocacy in the inspection process. We will pilot schemes to recruit advocates to visit homes before an inspection to help explain the process and prepare residents and clients for what they want to say. Also advocates will help people fill in pre-inspection questionnaires, if that's what people want.

We will look to recruit our own pool of advocates - possibly from our ex-lay inspectors. As with our paid inspectors, we will look to recruit advocates who reflect the make-up of the borough.

If people who use services already have their own advocates, we will look to liaise with them as appropriate.

during the inspection

standard 9   The style of inspection

We will carry out inspections in an informal, friendly, approachable but professional way. Our inspectors' main job is to talk to residents to find out what they think and to judge the quality of their lives. Inspection will only become a 'formal' process when it needs to.

Our inspectors will:
- chat with residents
- join in activities (including trips out) where appropriate and invited
- talk to staff in a relaxed way, allowing staff to do the talking
- be polite, approachable and respect the people and needs of all those around them

- fit the inspection around the working day and not expect it to be the other way around - except in special circumstances
- look to involve as many different people with an interest in the home as possible.

standard 10   The time taken by inspection

Our inspections will last only as long as they have to. Announced inspections should cover a whole day. In homes we will take steps to include night staff in the process.

standard 11   Using members of the public

We will do our best to make sure that a lay inspector is on every announced inspection and unannounced inspection, where possible. Meeting this standard depends on the availability of members of the public giving up their free time. However, we will look to recruit enough lay people to make this happen.

after the inspection

standard 12   Inspection reports

Our reports will be clear, well laid out and in simple, plain English. We will encourage inspectors to combine fact and opinion but will clearly identify the two. All our published reports will be aimed at the public. However, we will also publish reports aimed at residents and clients, and take into account the different needs of others.

standard 13   Delivery of inspection reports

We will deliver draft inspection reports within three weeks of our inspection being completed. A draft copy of the report will be sent to the home or centre and to their external managers or owners. Copies will be sent to others upon request. If asked to do so, our inspectors will come back and talk to you about the report they've written.

standard 14   Comments on inspection reports

You will be given four weeks to comment on the report. If you do not contact us in that time, we will send out a reminder giving you a final two week deadline. If still no response, the report will be published without your management response.

We will encourage comments on:
- getting our facts right
- any disagreements with opinions or comments we may have made
- any requirements and recommendations we may have made
- the way our inspectors carried out their job
- the report and inspection process generally.

standard 15   Publishing the report

We will try to publish your report within two months of the completed inspection. All reports are open to the public. They are made available from libraries, the unit itself and other places. Only childminder reports are not available from libraries.

standard 16   Following up reports

We will set in place a method to follow up any requirements or recommendations made in a report to check on your progress.

standard 17   Checking up on our performance

Our two Inspection Advisory Groups (one for adults' services, one for children's services) will be kept informed about how we are performing in meeting these standards. Homes and centres will be asked to judge us on these standards. We will look to recruit advocates to provide independent feedback from residents and clients.

appendix 2

people who took part in the research for this book

It is with great thanks that I list below all those people who took part in providing information for this book. The time taken to fill in yet another questionnaire (particularly an eight page one) is hugely appreciated. In the questionnaires respondents were asked if they would like to be credited for their involvement. Those who answered 'yes' are listed below. Thank you and to those who gave their names but wished to remain anonymous, and, finally, to those who remained completely anonymous.

providers

Mel Arundel	Assistant manager
Ray Barton	Owner/manager
Margaret P Bougard	Owner/manager
Beate Braban	Owner/manager
Cynthia Brown	Manager
Stella Cargill	Manager
Edward Carr	Manager
Elspeth Clark	Manager
Jo Clarke	Senior support worker
Mrs J F Collins	Owner/manager
Bob Compion	Manager
Angela Craigie	Manager
Sue Cross	Manager
Kate Cunningham	Manager
Carol Darkins	Manager
Carol Day	Manager
Bridget Donald	Manager
Jamesina Fern	Manager
Elizabeth Fowler	Manager
Sarah Friel	Manager
Mr S Gilbert	Manager
Elke Gilmore	Manager
P A Gray	Owner/manager
Mrs Laurel Green	Manager
Margaret Gruber	Manager
Rose Hannis	Manager
Carol Hill	Owner/manager
Mrs D Horan	Owner/manager
Jeni Hoyle	Manager
Virginia Ruth Hunt	Manager/lessee

B A Jones	Manager
Susan Kay	Manager
Mr D Laybourne	Owner/manager
Mrs D Laybourne	Owner/manager
Jean P A Lyon	Chief Executive
Val Marshall	Manager
Caroline Maxted	Owner/manager
Doreen McGee	Manager
Sam Moonoosamy	Manager
Frank Moulds	Manager
Jane Muir	Manager
Alan Paterson	Manager
Pat Petterson	Manager
Carol Phaup	Manager
Pam Purnell	Manager
R Purusram	Owner
Sylvie Rising	Manager
Cathy Robertson	Manager
Wendy Shap	Owner
Mrs Carole Simpson	Manager
Michael Smith	Manager
Joan Spendlove	Manager
Grant Steele	Owner
Barbara Thomas	Manager
Martin Thomas	Owner/manager
Carol Towse	Owner/manager
Carolyn Wallace	Manager
Mary Wiseman	Acting manager
Rod Wood	Manager
Jean Wright	Owner/manager

Fourteen providers gave their names but preferred not be credited by name, and 22 providers sent anonymous questionnaires.

inspection unit staff

Gill Ager	Principal Inspector
Mary Camacho	Head of Unit
Tony Clarke	Inspector
Samuel Doku	Head of Unit
Chris Doorly	Head of Unit
Elizabeth Findlay	Inspector
Bridget Forrest	Inspector
Bob Fox	Nursing Homes Adviser
Mark Goodman	Head of Unit
Jennie Guest	Head of Unit
Jan Johnston	Head of Unit
Janet G Jones	Inspector
Glenys Lloyd	Acting Head of Unit
Dan Mackay	Inspector

Helen McLoughlin	Inspector
Liz Norton	Head of Unit
Jo Palmer	Inspector
Keith Phillips	Head of Unit
John Rushforth	Inspector
Chris Stadames	Head of Unit
Deborah Sterry	Inspector
Mike Usher	Inspector
Irene Ward	Inspector
Elizabeth Whatley	Head of Unit

Fourteen inspectors gave their names but preferred not be credited by name, and four inspectors sent anonymous questionnaires.